Culture and the Politics of Welfare

Other Palgrave Pivot titles

Paula Loscocco: Phillis Wheatly's Miltonic Poetics

Mark Axelrod: Notions of the Feminine: Literary Essays from Dostoyevsky to Lacan

John Coyne and Peter Bell: The Role of Strategic Intelligence in Law Enforcement: Policing Transnational Organized Crime in Canada, the United Kingdom and Australia

Niall Gildea, Helena Goodwyn, Megan Kitching and Helen Tyson (editors): English Studies: The State of the Discipline, Past, Present and Future

Yoel Guzansky: The Arab Gulf States and Reform in the Middle East: Between Iran and the "Arab Spring"

Menno Spiering: A Cultural History of British Euroscepticism

Matthew Hollow: Rogue Banking: A History of Financial Fraud in Interwar Britain

Alexandra Lewis: Security, Clans and Tribes: Unstable Clans in Somaliland, Yemen and the Gulf of Aden

Sandy Schumann: How the Internet Shapes Collective Actions

Christy M. Oslund: Disability Services and Disability Studies in Higher Education: History, Contexts, and Social Impacts

Erika Mansnerus: Modelling in Public Health Research: How Mathematical Techniques Keep Us Healthy

William Forbes and Lynn Hodgkinson: Corporate Governance in the United Kingdom: Past, Present and Future

Michela Magliacani: Managing Cultural Heritage: Ecomuseums, Community Governance and Social Accountability

Sara Hsu and Nathan Perry: Lessons in Sustainable Development from Malaysia and Indonesia

Ted Newell: Five Paradigms for Education: Foundational Views and Key Issues

Sophie Body-Gendrot and Catherine Wihtol de Wenden: Policing the Inner City in France, Britain, and the US

William Sims Bainbridge: An Information Technology Surrogate for Religion: The Veneration of Deceased Family in Online Games

Anthony Ridge-Newman: Cameron's Conservatives and the Internet: Change, Culture and Cyber Toryism

Ian Budge and Sarah Birch: National Policy in a Global Economy: How Government Can Improve Living Standards and Balance the Books

Barend Lutz and Pierre du Toit: Defining Democracy in a Digital Age: Political Support on Social Media

Assaf Razin and Efraim Sadka: Migration States and Welfare States: Why Is America Different from Europe?

Conra D. Gist: Preparing Teachers of Color to Teach: Culturally Responsive Teacher Education in Theory and Practice

David Baker: Police, Picket-Lines and Fatalities: Lessons from the Past

palgrave▶pivot

Culture and the Politics of Welfare: Exploring Societal Values and Social Choices

John Hudson
University of York, UK

Nam Kyoung Jo
SungKongHoe University, South Korea

and

Antonia Keung
University of York, UK

© John Hudson, Nam Kyoung Jo, Antonia Keung 2015

All rights reserved. No reproduction, copy or transmission of this publication may be made without written permission.

No portion of this publication may be reproduced, copied or transmitted save with written permission or in accordance with the provisions of the Copyright, Designs and Patents Act 1988, or under the terms of any licence permitting limited copying issued by the Copyright Licensing Agency, Saffron House, 6–10 Kirby Street, London EC1N 8TS.

Any person who does any unauthorized act in relation to this publication may be liable to criminal prosecution and civil claims for damages.

The authors have asserted their rights to be identified as the authors of this work in accordance with the Copyright, Designs and Patents Act 1988.

First published 2015 by
PALGRAVE MACMILLAN

Palgrave Macmillan in the UK is an imprint of Macmillan Publishers Limited, registered in England, company number 785998, of Houndmills, Basingstoke, Hampshire RG21 6XS.

Palgrave Macmillan in the US is a division of St Martin's Press LLC, 175 Fifth Avenue, New York, NY 10010.

Palgrave Macmillan is the global academic imprint of the above companies and has companies and representatives throughout the world.

Palgrave® and Macmillan® are registered trademarks in the United States, the United Kingdom, Europe and other countries.

ISBN: 978–1–137–45750–9 EPUB
ISBN: 978–1–137–45749–3 PDF
ISBN: 978–1–137–45748–6 Hardback

A catalogue record for this book is available from the British Library.

A catalog record for this book is available from the Library of Congress.

www.palgrave.com/pivot

DOI: 10.1057/9781137457493

Contents

List of Figures	vi
List of Tables	vii
Acknowledgements	viii
Introduction	1
1 Exploring the Cultural Context of Welfare Policy Making	5
2 Exploring the Culture–Welfare Nexus: A Quantitative Comparative Analysis	24
3 Exploring the Culture–Welfare Nexus: A Qualitative Comparative Analysis	49
4 Exploring the Culture–Welfare Nexus: Key Trends, Key Cases	77
5 Conclusion: Bringing Culture 'Back In' to Comparative Social Policy Analysis	106
Bibliography	114
Index	125

List of Figures

1.1	The process for extracting examples of societal values	15
1.2	Cluster analysis of societal values data	20
3.1	Overview of three-step approach	56
3.2	Intermediate and proximate factors in the Social Democratic and Southern European regimes	60
3.3	Intermediate and proximate factors in the Liberal regime	62
3.4	Intermediate and proximate factors in the Conservative/Corporatist regime	65
4.1	Conservatism index scores by regime	84
4.2	Ireland's rapidly rising family policy expenditure	89
4.3	Traditional family values scores by country, over time	93
4.4	Raw EVS/WVS responses for components in traditional family values factor, Social Democratic countries versus whole sample average	96
4.5	Optimistic values scores by country, over time	101

List of Tables

1.1	Cluster analysis of societal values data	19
A1.1	Examples of societal values extracted	22
2.1	Correlations with social expenditure on unemployment	29
2.2	Prediction of social expenditure on unemployment	30
2.3	Prediction of share of social expenditure on unemployment	34
2.4	Correlations with social expenditure on family	37
2.5	Prediction of social expenditure on family policy	38
2.6	Prediction of share of social expenditure on family policy	41
2.7	Prediction the generosity of maternity leave FTE rates	43
3.1	Creating scores for QCA sets	51
3.2	Factors and outcomes in three-step fsQCA	53
4.1	Cluster analysis of societal values data for Conservative/Corporatist regime	79
4.2	Cluster analysis of societal values data for Conservative/Corporatist regime – conservative social norms; religiosity; traditional family values	81
4.3	Cluster analysis of societal values data for Liberal regime: conservative social norms; religiosity; traditional family values	86

Acknowledgements

We are grateful to the Economic and Social Research Council for financial support in pursuing this work (Award no: ES/J00460X/1). Without their support the project would not have been possible.

We could not have conducted our analysis without access to the quantitative data underpinning it: we are extremely grateful to have had access to data from EVS/WVS, OECD and excellent resources compiled by Klaus Armingeon's team and by our University of York colleague Stefan Kühner. We would like to thank Dominic Richardson at the OECD for providing access to data on family policy structures too.

Some early ideas from the project were presented at conferences. We are grateful to colleagues who provided feedback at the UK Social Policy Association Conference at the University of Sheffield; the Australian Social Policy Conference at the University of New South Wales; and, the Second International Conference on Social Policy and Governance at the Hong Kong Institute of Education.

We are also very grateful to colleagues at the University of York who provided helpful feedback on our project proposal and earlier drafts of this work, particularly Kate Brown, Naomi Finch, Dan Horsfall, Kathleen Kiernan and Stefan Kühner. All errors and omissions naturally remain our responsibility and not those of colleagues.

Finally, we would like to thank Palgrave Macmillan for commissioning the text and for their patient support during the process of bringing it to print.

Introduction

Hudson, John, Nam Kyoung Jo and Antonia Keung. *Culture and the Politics of Welfare: Exploring Societal Values and Social Choices.* Basingstoke: Palgrave Macmillan, 2015. DOI: 10.1057/9781137457493.0005.

This book has its origins in a conversation that began around ten years ago when two of us (John Hudson and Nam K. Jo) met for practically the first time and together pondered the foundations of social solidarity. More specifically, we wondered why some societies seemed to be more disposed towards the support of pro-welfare state political parties than others and, in particular, why such parties often seemed to struggle to gain traction among the electorate. This, in turn, reflected curiosity about the dominance of the right in our countries (the United Kingdom and South Korea, respectively) that had resulted in both of us looking outwards at other countries in order to help better understand our own. Over time this topic of discussion gradually evolved into a set of research projects examining societal values – as a proxy for national cultures – and their impact on welfare state politics. We were lucky to be joined for the work presented here by our colleague Antonia Keung who brought not only great methodological expertise to the project but also a great knowledge of policy areas excluded from our earlier work. The work presented here is a collective effort drawing on the contribution of all three of us.

The core of the text is broken into four chapters. In Chapter 1, we outline the theoretical context for our work. We highlight the often-implicit role the notion of culture plays in debates about cross-national differences in welfare. We critique culturally deterministic approaches, favouring models of social policy-making that view culture as a significant but not decisive influence on welfare. However, we suggest that much work in this sphere is constrained by what we might loosely describe as either macro- or micro-level conceptions of culture. The macro-level approach views cultural/ideological traditions as a force filtering policy decisions by constraining policy options to those that are in accordance with the dominant cultural/ideological traditions of each nation. Meanwhile, in the micro-level approach, the role played by public opinion in policy-making is the main focal point, with empirical work based on the analysis of micro-level survey data. We suggest that an 'in-between level' approach is possible that falls between these macro- and micro-level approaches, in which the focus is on the empirical analysis of stable societal values. We round off the chapter by using our in-between approach to examine four waves of European Values Study (EVS) and the World Values Survey (WVS) in order to extract examples of societal values on which we build-in the remainder of the text.

In Chapter 2, we report findings from a series of regression models exploring how far the cultural context helps us to understand cross-national variations in social policy provision. More specifically, we explore how far the cultural context helps us to understand variations in key policy inputs associated with traditional social risks (we use unemployment policy as our main example) and variation in policy responses to new social risks (using family policy as our main example). Our quantitative analysis provides strong support for the 'culture matters' thesis, with the inclusion of societal values in the regression models almost always clearly improving their explanatory power. We highlight too the particular significance of some societal values in creating a 'pro-welfare' context and consider why some values seem to boost welfare effort and others diminish it. However, we also note some limitations inherent in our approach, pointing to the limits of a regression-based analysis that is to a considerable degree data-driven and based upon a modest overall number of observations.

In Chapter 3, we 'drill down' below the big picture provided by our regression models. We use fuzzy-set qualitative comparative analysis (fsQCA) in order to do so, it being a particularly useful method when investigators have a modestly sized sample and where they wish to explore the impact of *combinations* of factors on an outcome. We develop a new application of the approach we dub a 'three-step model' that allows us to disentangle long-, medium- and short-term influences on policy differences. We place a specific emphasis on trying to explore what appear to be potentially important interactions between key examples of societal values and welfare regimes: so, for example, we explore how the influence of strong traditional family values on family policy might vary by welfare regime or how its influence might be contingent on the presence of other societal values such as a high degree of religiosity. However, we also note that fsQCA methods have their own limits. Indeed, they are ultimately designed to help researchers bridge parsimonious big picture analyses and more detailed case-based analyses and, in so doing, to sharpen conceptual thinking by creating an ongoing dialogue between parsimonious theorising and more detailed case study analysis. Consequently, we flag interesting cases that seem worthy of more detailed analysis. This sets the context for our final substantive chapter.

In Chapter 4, we focus, in more detail, on some of the key trends and key cases that Chapters 2 and 3 suggested may be of particular interest. More specifically, we examine four issues: the Conservative/Corporatist regime puzzle; the Liberal regime bifurcation; the meaning of traditional family values; and, the significance of optimistic values. In exploring these issues we demonstrate how more detailed exploration of case study evidence may help understand how the culture-welfare nexus operates in practice, offering a more nuanced perspective than is possible through broad-brushed macro-level comparisons alone. We also explore some of the methodological challenges uncovered in Chapters 2 and 3, pointing to refinements to our approach that may be taken forward in future research.

Finally, in Chapter 5, we summarise the core arguments advanced in the book as a whole before taking stock of our contribution and the future research agendas suggested by our analysis. We suggest that there are strong reasons for bringing culture 'back in' to the comparative analysis of welfare states and that advances in data collection and data analysis mean that there will be still greater potential for fruitful analysis in the future.

1
Exploring the Cultural Context of Welfare Policy Making

Abstract: *After reviewing debates on the role of culture in shaping cross-national variations in social policy, we argue that culture is best viewed as a significant but not decisive influence on patterns of welfare. We argue that empirical analysis has been somewhat constrained by conceptions of culture that are either too broad or too narrow, offering an 'in-between approach' that identifies stable patterns of societal values that we suggest can act as useful proxy measures for the cultural context of policy making. Examining European Values Study/World Values Survey data covering a period from 1981 to 2009 we identify eight examples of societal values on which we build in the remainder of the book.*

Keywords: culture; societal values; welfare state models

Hudson, John, Nam Kyoung Jo and Antonia Keung. *Culture and the Politics of Welfare: Exploring Societal Values and Social Choices.* Basingstoke: Palgrave Macmillan, 2015. DOI: 10.1057/9781137457493.0006.

Exploring culture and welfare

It is commonly claimed that culture matters in welfare, not least because social policies are based on the shared answers to normative questions such as why someone should care about others?, who deserves our care? and what should be done by governments?, the answers to which reflect diverse understandings of human nature that are shaped by different values systems in different countries and at different times (Deacon, 2002: 1; Marshall, 1972; Titmuss, 1974: 49; van Oorschot, 2000). Indeed, key theorists who have examined the links between culture and welfare have suggested that widely and deeply embedded cultural values form a key context for social policy making and are likely to be a significant factor in explaining cross-national variations in welfare (Pfau-Effinger, 2005). To this end, comparative social policy analysts have shown a growing interest in questions around culture in recent years and a paper by Pfau-Effinger (2005) published in the *Journal of Social Policy* is, at the time of writing, among the top ten most cited papers in the journal's history with over 200 citations according to Google Scholar.[1] On the whole, however, culture remains an issue largely dealt with in passing – or implicitly – in comparative analyses of welfare, with relatively little attention paid to how culture relates to the commonly cited welfare regimes or models of welfare that underpin much comparative welfare states research.

The absence of extensive empirical investigation of such issues has been partly due to the limited availability of data on cultural dimensions, but difficulties in operationalising culture empirically have also played a role. Recent developments have addressed both of these issues directly. The European Values Study (EVS) and the World Values Survey (WVS) now provide us with detailed quantitative data on values stretching back over several decades with more than four waves of each having been completed spanning a period from 1981 to 2009. As importantly, detailed debates about how this data might be analysed in order to identify proxy measures of culture have provided us with established methodological approaches on which to build. Indeed, in an earlier work we (Jo, 2011) provided a key contribution to the recent literature in this regard basing our approach on the analysis of stable societal values.

In this chapter we review debates on the role culture plays in shaping cross-national differences in welfare. In so doing, we draw out key conceptual themes found within the literature on culture and welfare and, in so doing, also outline the distinctive contribution provided by our own analytic and methodological frameworks. Building on this work we then examine EVS and WVS data in order to extract examples of societal values that might act as a useful proxy for culture and, in turn, facilitate empirical explorations of welfare-culture linkages. We round off the chapter by demonstrating these examples of societal values operate independently from commonly identified 'welfare regimes' and so merit separate inclusion in analytic models seeking to explain cross-national variations in welfare.

Culture and models of welfare

The 'welfare modelling business' (Abrahamson, 1999) has been at the heart of comparative social policy analysis since the publication of Esping-Andersen's (1990) path-breaking *The Three Worlds of Welfare Capitalism* and attempts to classify welfare states continue to command much attention (see Abrahamson, 2011; Powell and Barrientos, 2011). Indeed, with the increased availability of reliable comparative data from bodies such as the OECD (Castles, 2002) and a continual refinement of classificatory methods (see Hudson and Kühner, 2010), it is hardly surprising that there should be a lively and ongoing debate nearly 25 years after Esping-Andersen's classic first appeared in print. We will not rehearse the basics of the welfare regimes debate here (but see Arts and Gellisen (2002), Abrahamson (1999; 2011) and Powell and Barrientos (2011) for overviews), other than to note that the core theme from this literature is broadly supported by many comparative scholars: that each nation's welfare system on balance reflects a long-term historical path of development and that distinctive paths of development exist that reflect the outcome of complex long-term social, political and economic processes in which historical-institutional forces play a key role in fostering the path-dependence of welfare systems (Abrahamson, 1999; Esping-Andersen, 1990). As hinted above, culture has played a largely implicit role in these debates, though it has also been suggested that culture can foster the path-dependence of welfare systems[2] (Jo, 2011; Pfau-Effinger, 2004a; van Oorschot, 2006: 24); for instance, deeply embedded cultural values can bolster support for existing social provisions if the two are well matched. Indeed, in reflecting on the longue durée of policy, Pierson (2004: 39) notes that there can be significant positive feedback effects at play that reinforce dominant ideas in a society over time, meaning collective understandings in a society may be path-dependent too.³ How, then, have key theorists in the welfare typologies debate approached questions of culture?

In his ground breaking *The Three Worlds of Welfare Capitalism* Esping-Andersen (1990) made two passing references to culture (Esping-Andersen, 1990: 13 and 191), but there were no substantive references to questions of culture despite the fact that his three welfare regime types are presumed to be fundamentally shaped by 'the historical legacy of regime institutionalization' (Esping-Andersen, 1990: 29). This might be regarded as something of an omission, particularly given that some of the factors he placed under the umbrella phrase 'historical legacy of regime institutionalization' might be viewed as cultural influences: for instance, with respect to the conservative/corporatist regime he (1990: 27) suggested the influence of the Church and a related commitment to preserving 'traditional familyhood' were key. His follow-up text (*Social Foundations of Post-Industrial Economies*) offered few additional clues, though a footnote talked of 'a culture of universalistic solidarities' in Scandinavian societies (Esping-Andersen, 1999: 78).

However, his edited collection *Welfare States in Transition* – published in-between the two solo contributions highlighted above (Esping-Andersen, 1996a) – is interesting insofar as some of the contributors explicitly highlighted culture as a key factor in understanding welfare state types. For instance, Castles (1996: 111, emphasis added), based on his analysis of Australia and New Zealand, noted that 'Policy options are broadly shaped by the economic forces and social and *cultural structures* which shape a generation's dilemmas and opportunities', while Goodman and Peng (1996: 193, emphasis added) suggested that East Asian welfare states such as Japan, South Korea and Taiwan had developed on the basis of seeking 'solutions from within [their] own *traditional cultural framework* rather than adapting Western patterns'. Indeed, Esping-Andersen (1996b: x, emphasis added) observed in the introduction to the book that the different regions examined within it are 'quite distinct in terms of *cultural and political legacies*, economic development, and shared social policy traditions'. Perhaps one of the reasons *Welfare States in Transition* gave culture a more prominent role is that it embraced perspectives, and cases, that featured heavily in early challenges to the trichotomous classification of welfare regime ideal types outlined in *The Three Worlds of Welfare*. Hence, for instance, Castles' (1996) chapter built directly on his work with Mitchell (Castles and Mitchell, 1993) that argued Australia and New Zealand were misclassified by Esping-Andersen as liberal regimes because key features such as redistribution through collective bargaining had been missed despite their centrality to these distinctive 'wage earners welfare states'. Meanwhile, the chapter by Goodman and Peng (1996) built on, among others, Jones' (1990, 1993) suggestion that a distinctive 'Confucian' model of welfare could be found in East Asia in which values distinctive from those found in 'Western' countries lead to a welfare system that is also distinct. What is interesting here is not only that both of these strands sparked important debates about the existence of an additional and distinctive welfare regime in their region (see Arts and Gellisen, 2002), but also that in both instances culture was seen as a *central* factor in understanding distinct welfare state types.

Castles (1998; see also Castles and Mitchell, 1993) ultimately offered a rival set of welfare types based on: 'the identification of differences between groups of nations defined in terms of common cultural, historical and geographical nations [termed] 'families of nations' [...] which correspond substantially to the borders of what appear to be *quite clearly identified cultural zones*' (Castles, 1998: 8, emphasis added). In other words, he placed culture centre stage in *defining* welfare state clusters. Many of those involved in driving the East Asian welfare model thesis took a similar approach, Jones' (1990; 1993) arguing a common core of Confucian beliefs underpinned a distinct model of welfare while Rieger and Liebfried have suggested that 'Confucian culture can be identified as the fundamental cause of an independent path of welfare state evolution in East Asia' (2003: 243).

However, despite these important strands of debate, it is fair to say that the ways in which culture and welfare regimes interact or intersect is relatively underexplored. Moreover, it should be noted that the culturally deterministic approaches espoused by those such as Jones (1990, 1993) are now generally eschewed (Hudson, Kühner and Yang, 2014): with respect to claims about a culturally rooted East Asian welfare model, for instance, critics have pointed to the diversity of social policy frameworks found in the region (see e.g., Jacobs, 2000 Peng, 2002; Ramesh and Asher 2000; Walker and Wong, 2005; White and Goodman, 1998), with Kwon (1998: 27) concluding that cultural-historical approaches are relatively 'weak in explaining the precise national profiles of social policy and differences between welfare systems' in the region.

More nuanced contributions to the debate on culture and welfare dispense with culturally deterministic perspectives altogether and instead see culture as *one* of the factors that might interplay with other forces in shaping social policy. For instance, in Pfau-Effinger's (2005; cf. 2004b: 37–61) 'welfare culture approach' the impact of culture on welfare policy making is mediated by a social system, her model recognising the roles of political actors, social structures and institutions in policy making. This is a more sophisticated model altogether, and its reasoning naturally leads to the admission that cultural dimensions are not the sole determinants of social policy (Deacon, 2002: 8; Pfau-Effinger, 2005: 11) and are probably less influential than economic and political factors (van Oorschot and Halman, 2000: 21).[4]

Conceptualising culture

Underpinning these different arguments about the ways in which culture and welfare influence each other are implicit differences in how culture is conceptualised. Indeed, studies exploring the links between culture and social policy generally fall into two broad camps in terms of how they conceptualise culture.

The first approach – most commonly found in more long-range historical analyses - views cultural/ideological traditions as a macro-level force filtering policy decisions in a manner that constrains policy options to those that are in accordance with the dominant cultural/ideological traditions of each nation (e.g., Castles, 1998: 52–58; O'Connor and Robinson, 2008; Stjernø, 2008; van Kersbergen, 1995; van Kersbergen and Kremer, 2008; van Kersbergen and Manow, 2009). From within this tradition Opielka (2008) talks of 'cultural institutionalism', viewing religion as the foundation of differing social systems, and Lockhart (2001) explains the origins of institutional differences by reference to a series of cultural types. The conception of the effect of culture in this camp is broad and comprehensive, with a dominant tradition understood as having shaped not only social policy but also broader social structures. However, as Stjernø (2008: 55) notes, there is a risk that very broad conceptions of culture such as this offer overly abstract explanations of the impact of culture that are focused on 'post hoc explanation'. Moreover, there are good reasons to doubt whether just one or two fundamental cultural dimensions can capture the complexity of the real world (Lockhart, 2001: 227–228). In short, while these macro approaches can illuminate the cultural foundations of welfare, their generality means they are less useful in facilitating the concrete analysis of the role of culture in shaping the specifics of welfare state activity in particular contexts.

At the opposite pole, the second approach focuses on the exploration of micro-level data regarding public opinion about welfare related issues. Here the role played by public opinion in policy making is the main focal point of both theoretical (Burstein, 1998) and empirical (Page and Shapiro, 1983) analyses, key studies highlighting the role it plays in setting the agenda, constraining policy choices and legitimising policy decisions (Cnaan et al., 1993; Pfau-Effinger, 2005; van Oorschot, 2006). Empirical investigations within this tradition have pointed to distinctive welfare attitudes across countries regarding issues such 'welfare responsibility' (Gundelach, 1994), the appropriate scope of welfare state interventions (Andreβ and Heien, 2001; Svallfors, 1997, 2007), the desired extent of social support for the unemployed (Blekesaune and Quadagno, 2003), as well as of perceptions of the cause of poverty (van Oorschot and Halman, 2000) and deservingness of welfare target groups (van Oorschot, 2000, 2006). While this approach has successfully facilitated empirical analyses of the cultural dimension in relation to welfare, it has been less successful in identifying causal impacts of welfare attitudes on social policy. The temporal instability of public opinion is the major stumbling point here; as Gelissen (2008: 247) notes, public opinion is influenced by 'the immediate surrounding socio-economic conditions'. For instance, how deserving the unemployed are viewed to be is affected by the unemployment rate (van Oorschot, 2006). We might also note that policy makers can influence public opinion (Page et. al., 1987) and that opinion survey findings can be sensitive to the specifics of the welfare context addressed in survey questions too. In short, attitudes uncovered in public opinion surveys simply too often lack the long-term stability required in order to be deemed indicators of broad cultural values.

In between these two camps, our own contribution to this debate (Jo, 2011) outlined the potential for an alternative conception of culture based on 'in-between analysis' that is both more specific and more clearly empirically rooted than the abstract approach of the first camp but has advantages over the second approach because it distinguishes the analysis of stable values from the analysis of fluctuating public opinion. This, we suggest, offers an empirically and conceptually robust route to analysing the impact of culture on welfare: one where culture and the social system are interrelated but not decisively determined by each other, where the relationship between culture, actors and the social system is an interactive and iterative one. This tallies with the 'welfare culture approach' advocated by Pfau-Effinger (2005; cf. 2004b: 37–61). In this perspective, the cultural system and the social system interrelate and interplay, mainly through social actors whose ideas and interests are shaped by each, with social policy the outcome of this interplay. In short, our 'in-between level' analysis conceptualises culture as the cultural context for policy making and is able to facilitate quantitatively rooted cross-national analyses based in such a presumption (Jo, 2011).

The in-between approach: identifying stable societal values

Hofstede (2001: 9–11) has argued that if the cultural context is stable then we can usefully focus on *values* as a key cultural dimension. In conceptual terms, values are trans-situational and more immutable than attitudes (Hitlin and Piliavin, 2004), representing the most lasting ideas regarding what is desirable and ultimately affecting attitudes (Aalberg, 2003: 5–8). As with culture as a whole, this sub-concept of culture might be viewed to operate at different levels. Indeed, Haller (2002: 143) distinguishes between three kinds of values: universal values that must be equivalent to the basic human values in Psychology (e.g., see Schwartz, 1992); 'societal values' which are more concrete and 'valid in a specific societal context'; and 'situational values' which are related to 'the concrete application of values to social behaviour in specific circumstances'. We suggest that societal values represent an 'in-between level' of this sub-concept of culture, operating between concrete public opinion and abstract basic human values. Societal values are expected to vary more greatly across societies than universal values because they contain 'references to concrete social circumstances' (Haller, 2002: 143) but at the same time are more deeply embedded within a society and more stable than situational values. To this end, the analysis of aggregated micro-level data on societal values holds the potential for capturing the cultural context of policy making.

Crucially, the existence of successive waves of the EVS and the WVS contain detailed quantitative data on values stretching back over several decades with more than four waves of each having been completed during a period spanning from 1981 to 2009. Although the sample size for each country at each wave is not large (mostly between 1,000 and 1,500), particularly for an attitudinal survey, there are few cross-cultural surveys focusing on values and attitudes and fewer still with data for a relatively long period and wide range of countries. There have been few criticisms of the sample quality of these data, especially for the high-income countries which are the focus of the welfare state types debate we focus on here (Larsen, 2006: 27). In short, the EVS/WVS provide us with sufficient cross-national micro-level of data on values in order to identify societal values shared by the majority of the population in a large number of countries. In order to meet our 'in-between level' definition of values, however, we need to pinpoint values that are stable within individual countries over time and are independent of economic and political context. Here 'stability' does not mean immutability. As flagged above, our approach is rooted in a view of a cultural system existing alongside a social system where both influence the other in an iterative fashion. Consequently, the cultural context should be conceived as being 'dynamically stable' rather than being fixed and immutable (Oyserman and Uskul, 2008: 149–150). We suggest that, in practical terms, this means that any attempt to identify societal values using EVS and WVS data should not look for scores that are static but instead deploy dynamically stable scores of measures on the basis that cultural differences should be relatively enduring (Hitlin and Piliavin, 2004; Inglehart, 1990).

In an earlier piece of work (Jo, 2011) we developed a method for doing using EVS and corresponding WVS data that entailed looking at the persistence of differences in the cultural context between societies in order to draw examples of stable societal values from all three waves of the EVS and corresponding WVS data available at that time (1981/1982, 1990 and 1999/2000), examining data for 22 OECD countries with established welfare states in so doing. In order to allow for the stability of items to be tested, only questions repeatedly asked in all three waves of EVS/WVS were selected for examination and these were then filtered again by data availability, which left us with 83 items. Based on correlations ten groups emerged and each group was factor analysed with the pooled dataset. These factor solutions were compared with those from the data by each wave, each country and both in order to test comparability of underlying factors across time and country (van de Vijver et al., 2008) and in this process it was found that many notions not only differed across countries but also changed over time. Comparable latent factors were extracted through an iterative process of discarding items containing incomparable notions and re-analysis. Following van de Vijver et al. (2008) comparability of extracted underlying dimensions across levels (i.e., individual and country levels) was tested. The individual level values and the country level values can have differing internal logics and be different (Hofstede, 2001; Schwartz, 1994), so this process is key in terms of testing whether our extracted factors are meaningful examples of underlying values found at both individual and country levels. There was a further drop of items following this. Finally, stability of the cultural context was examined by looking at how stable the differences in cultural context between societies were over time; drawing on Hofstede (2001) the correlation between ranks of countries by the means of underlying values at 1981/1982 and at 1999/2000 was examined in order to do this.[5] Figure 1.1. provides an overview of this process.

Based on the above approach, in our original study we (Jo, 2011) found six examples of societal values that were comparable across time and countries, cross-level equivalent and, when aggregated, stable over time in terms of their differences between societies: religiosity; traditional ethical values; legal permissiveness; tolerance; traditional family values; and, optimism. We then proceeded to explore the impact of these examples of societal values on welfare systems (van Oorschot, 2007: 134–135; cf. Pfau-Effinger, 2005). In order to capture the broader social, economic and political context of policy making, and the specifics of social policy activity, in this stage of the analysis data from the EVS/WVS was supplemented with data from the OECD SOCX database, the 'Comparative Welfare Reform Dataset 1960–2001' (Kühner, 2007a) and the 'Comparative Political Data Set 1960–2005' (Armingeon et al., 2008), along with data on welfare regime types drawn from Arts and Gelissen's (2002) summary of this literature.

In undertaking the analysis we found some strong indicators of the link between the cultural context and welfare (Jo, 2011: 12–16). For instance, public opinion on the causes of poverty appeared to be strongly dependent upon cultural context. Indeed, our regression models exploring perceptions of the causes of poverty were vastly improved by the addition of data on societal values. Substantively, we found in particular that societies with stronger religiosity were more likely to emphasise the role of an individual's actions in explaining poverty. Similarly, we also found that the proportion of social expenditure allocated to unemployment spending was linked to the cultural context, with our regression models again being greatly improved by the addition of cultural variables. Substantively we found that unemployment spending was likely to be allocated a higher share of social spending in societies where optimism and tolerance were more strongly embedded.

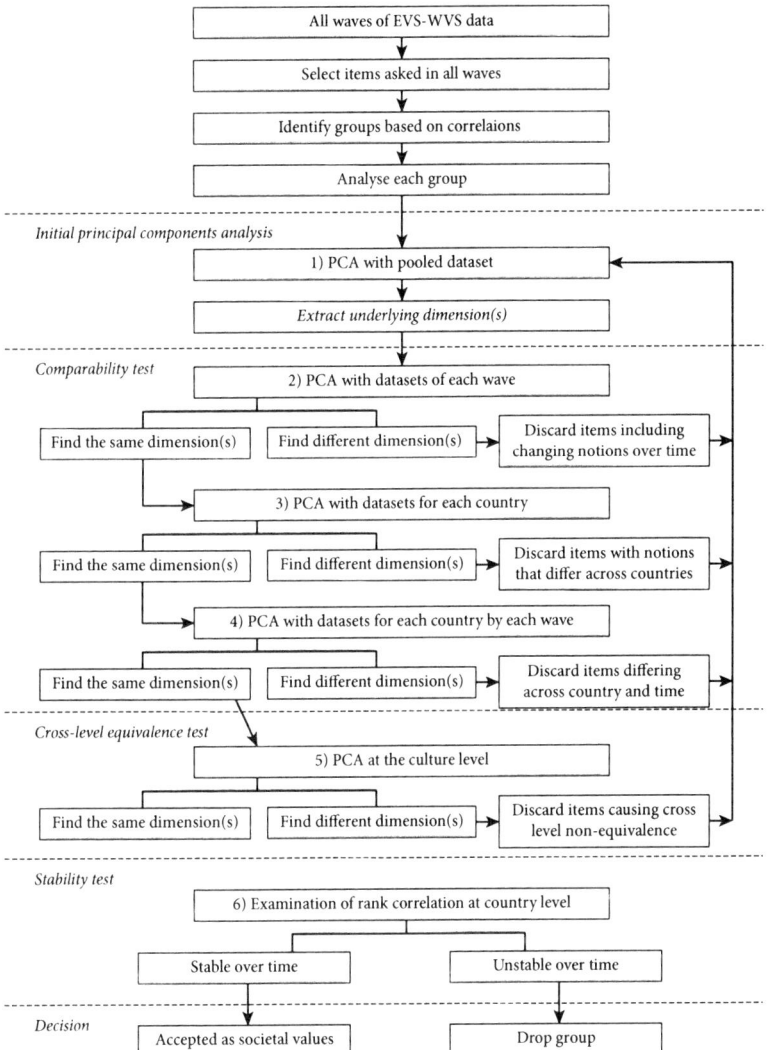

FIGURE 1.1   *The process for extracting examples of societal values*

Despite these strong examples of links between welfare and cultural context found in our earlier work (Jo, 2011), and suggestions from scholars exploring related themes that the examination of culture at the in-between level of societal values is a fruitful avenue (Busemeyer, 2013), there were nonetheless some important limitations within our earlier work. Data limitations placed some rather specific constraints on our analysis. For instance, though the values data stretched back over two decades, a longer time frame would have improved our certainty that stable values had been extracted. The subsequent release of an additional wave of both the EVS and WVS has provided us with an opportunity to test the robustness of our earlier findings. It is to this task that we now turn.

The cultural context revisited: identifying societal values

The starting point for our new analysis was to repeat the procedure outlined in Figure 1.1 for the identification of societal values but including data from the latest waves of the EVS and WVS. While the original study examined data from 1981/1982 to 1999/2000, the latest releases extend this until 2009. We also took this opportunity to expand our sample, extracting data on societal values from a broader range of countries. In total, this provided us with 173 societal level cases (counting countries by time point separately), covering some 59 countries at a maximum of four time points each and 243,976 individual cases. The initial analysis extracted 11 factors.[6] Subsequent exploration reduced this to eight examples of societal values, two more than found in our original study (Jo, 2011). Though there was a good degree of overlap in the extracted examples when compared to our earlier study we also found some slight variations in their composition and so use slightly varying labels for some of the overlapping societal values. These are:

- Religiosity: capturing the depth of attachment to religious institutions and the strength of faith in God and religion.
- Conservative social norms: capturing how socially illiberal societies are around issues such as divorce, abortion, sexuality and euthanasia.
- Permissive values on adherence to laws: capturing the extent to which the flouting of laws is seen as acceptable, for example, cheating on taxes, accepting bribes, claiming benefits fraudulently.
- Optimistic values: capturing the degree to which people in a society have a positive outlook and feel in control of their lives.
- Traditional family values: capturing the degree to which the nuclear family based around marriage is valued.

▶ Inter-personal tolerance: capturing the extent to which people in a society are tolerant of living next door to groups sometimes seen as difficult, deviant or problematic such as drug addicts, convicted criminals or emotionally unstable people.

In addition, we found two sets of values around what we might loosely term notions of *political participation and citizenship* that we have labelled:

▶ Political activeness: capturing the extent to which participation in political activities (beyond voting) such as demonstrating, signing petitions or joining unofficial strikes is a feature of the society.
▶ Political orientedness: capturing the extent to which people in a society show an interest in politics and discuss political matters with friends.

Table A1.1 provides an overview of all the input items from EVS/WVS that each of these factors is based on.

We should note that there are limitations in our approach arising from the fact that it is data driven and so the examples of societal values extracted decisively depend on the items covered by our survey data. The EVS and WVS are the most extensive international attitudinal surveys in terms of a focus on the values of people but this does not alter the fact that the findings from this method are always merely some *examples* of societal values that are dataset-biased and not exhaustive. In addition, we might also note that the factors themselves require conceptually rooted interpretation in order to create qualitative labels for them. Though for some factors a straightforward interpretation is possible based on the values they comprise (religiosity for instance) for others interpretation is more complex and contestable, meaning alternative labels may be more apposite (inter-personal tolerance for instance might be alternatively labelled as something lower order such as 'open-minded neighbourliness'). Nonetheless, the extracted societal values provide us with a useful base on which to explore ways in which the cultural context impacts on welfare and, crucially, open up numerous possibilities for undertaking quantitatively rooted analyses of the impact of culture on welfare policy be it through traditional regression style techniques or less well known approaches gaining traction in comparative analysis such Qualitative Comparative Analysis (QCA) (Rihoux and Ragin, 2008; see also, Hudson and Kühner, 2013). Having outlined the examples of societal values we are utilising, we round off the chapter by demonstrating that while these values overlap with the commonly cited groupings of welfare state types but are sufficiently different to be viewed as operating independently from them. This is important, for our theoretical model outlined above presumes culture and welfare systems influence each other in an iterative fashion – while also interacting with political, economic and social factors – which means that we should expect some close relation between welfare types and societal values but should not expect them to overlap fully. We then, in subsequent chapters, move on to explore how the societal values data can be used to explore the impact of culture on welfare policy making.

The embeddedness of culture in welfare types

A simple way of exploring whether culture operates independently from welfare types is to examine how far our examples of societal values overlap with commonly cited welfare types. If shared cultural foundations are key in determining different models of welfare then the clusters of both ought to be broadly similar. If, however, culture operates independently from welfare regimes/types then the picture should be more mixed. One simple way of exploring this is to perform a cluster analysis using all of our examples of societal values. We used Ward's method with values standardised as Z-scores. We included 23 countries commonly included in welfare typologies and, for each societal value, used the latest year for which factor scores were available for each example of societal values for each case.[7]

Table 1.1 presents the outcomes of the analysis, grouping countries by cluster and listing the commonly cited welfare types alongside each case. One challenge here, of course, is that typologies – and memberships within typologies – are contested (Arts and Gellisen, 2002). Based on our reading of the literature, guided by Arts and Gellisen (2002), the third column of Table 1.1 provides our view on where these cases are most commonly classified, but in column four we also list common alternatives. We should note that this does not mean that we agree with these common classifications: for instance, we include the East Asian type because it aids our exploration of the more deterministic analyses of culture and welfare but are highly sceptical about claims that an East Asian model exists (Hudson, Kühner and Yang, 2014; Jo, 2013). All told this gives us five welfare types: the conservative/corporatist, liberal and social democratic regimes identified by Esping-Andersen plus the

TABLE 1.1   *Cluster analysis of societal values data*

Cluster	Cases	Assumed welfare type	Common alternatives
1	Austria	Conservative/corporatist	
	Switzerland	Liberal	Conservative/corporatist[a]
	Germany	Conservative/corporatist	
	United Kingdom	Liberal	Radical[b]
	Luxembourg	Conservative/corporatist	
	Netherlands	Conservative/corporatist	Social democratic[c]
2	Australia	Liberal	Radical
	Canada	Liberal	
	Denmark	Social democratic	
	Finland	Social democratic	
	Norway	Social democratic	
	New Zealand	Liberal	Radical
	United States	Liberal	
3	Belgium	Conservative/corporatist	
	Spain	South European	
	France	Conservative/corporatist	
	Sweden	Social democratic	
4	Greece	South European	
	Ireland	Liberal	
	Italy	South European	Conservative/corporatist[d]
	Portugal	South European	
5	Japan	East Asian	Conservative/corporatist[e]
	South Korea	East Asian	

Notes: [a] Arts and Gelissen (2002: table 2) read Esping-Andersen as classifying Switzerland in the conservative type, but in a footnote to a regression model in Esping-Andersen (1999: 77) suggests it falls in the liberal type (see Hudson, 2012: 12).
[b] Australia, New Zealand and UK all classified as radical in Castles and Mitchell (1993), distinguishing them from Liberal cases such as the USA.
[c] We should note that Arts and Gelissen (2002: table 2) read Esping-Andersen as classifying the Netherlands in the social democratic type but its often a contested case and is undefined in Wildeboer Schut et al. (2001).
[d] Esping-Andersen, of course, did not include a Southern European cluster (Italy being the only case from the sub-region in his analysis), placing it within the conservative/corporatist cluster. In suggesting this additional type, Ferrera (1996) placed Italy firmly within it.
[e] Esping-Andersen, of course, did not include an East Asian cluster (Japan being the only case from the sub-region in his analysis), placing it within the conservative/corporatist cluster. Many of those suggesting this additional type placed Japan firmly within it though critics often note its dissimilarity with other welfare systems in the region.

Southern European (Ferrera, 1996) and East Asian (Rieger and Liebfried, 2003) types. To allow for ease of comparison we have interpreted our cluster analysis as having identified five groupings, though we should note that the distance between Clusters 1 and 2 is modest and that an

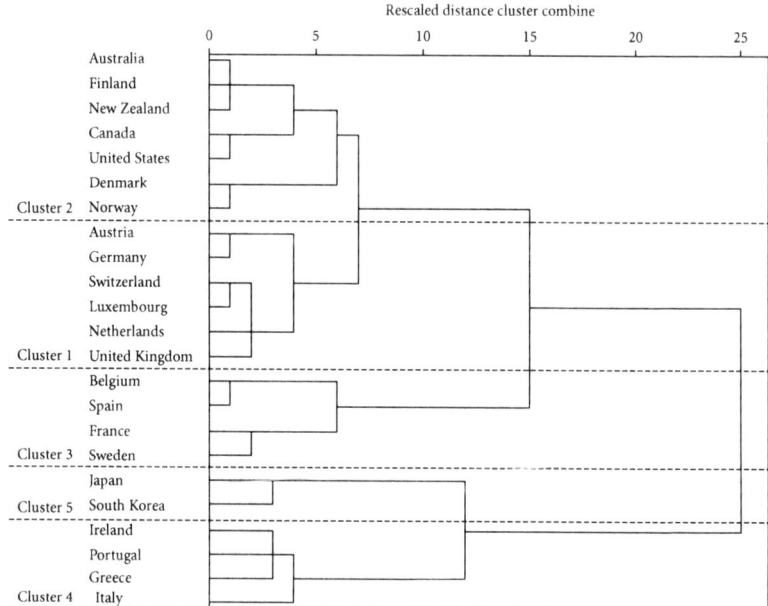

FIGURE 1.2   Cluster analysis of societal values data (dendrogram using ward linkage).

alternative reading would be that they should form a single cluster (as can be seen from the dendrogram in Figure 1.2).

Though arguably a somewhat crude approach, cluster analysis is commonly used by scholars trying to identify welfare types (e.g., Powell and Barrientos, 2004). The results of the cluster analysis suggest at best a modest overlap between the patterns of societal values and common welfare type memberships, with most clusters contain at least two examples of at least two welfare types and Cluster 1 being very diverse if we use the alternate welfare type classifications. The clear exception is Cluster 5 which comprises only East Asian cases, though given our data set only contains data on two cases in the region it may not capture the full diversity of values there.[8] Or, alternatively, it may be that the East Asian 'model' of welfare has been mistakenly identified as a welfare state type rather than a cultural 'type'. This would chime with our previous suggestion (Jo, 2013) that there is a coherence in terms of values in these two cases (Japan and South Korea) but that this does not translate into a common model of social policy. Further support for the conclusion that welfare types and our examples of societal values are weakly associated comes from manual inspection of the data for our examples of societal values by welfare regime type: though the patterns vary by each of the examples of societal values, in the round data plots underline that there is often considerable range within each welfare regime type with respect to the scores for each societal value. So, for instance, while some loose patterns are discernable (e.g., inter-personal tolerance is lower in the East Asia type than elsewhere or that permissive values on adherence to laws are more evident in Conservative and South European types) on the whole the picture defies simple explanation. Moreover, there are instances where the variation in scores *within* a type is as telling as variation in scores between types: for example, there is a wide (and skewed) range of scores for religiosity in the Liberal type and in traditional family values in the Conservative type.[9]

In short, there is at best only very limited support for the notion that culture and welfare state types are heavily connected. Indeed, there is good reason to presume the two are related but act independently of each other, providing a strong rationale for including societal values in analysis of welfare alongside indicators of welfare state type.

Chapter summary

This chapter makes three key points:

- In debates about cross-national variations in welfare, culture is often said to be an important factor in explaining difference, and has featured as an important explanatory factor in core contributions to the welfare types debate. However, its impact on varying policy structures has rarely been subjected to detailed empirical analysis, with its significance often implied or tied to crude deterministic accounts.
- In part, the relative paucity of studies is a result of complexities in conceptualising culture and developing robust 'measures' that can act as a proxy for culture in empirical analysis. We suggest that our 'in-between' approach that uses examples of societal values as a proxy for culture can address both these issues and open up extensive opportunities for empirical analysis of the impact of culture on welfare.
- Our examples of societal values do not merely capture the commonly identified welfare state types by another route, with scores for our societal values being only loosely related to common

welfare type memberships. There is good reason to presume the two are related but act independently of each other, providing a strong rationale for including societal values in cross-national analyses of welfare.

Having argued that there are good reasons to include societal values in cross-national analyses of welfare and shown how it is possible to do so, in the following two chapters we move onto this task, beginning with traditional quantitative approaches and then utilising QCA techniques. In so doing, we aim to explore the ways in which the culture context of policy making impacts on cross-national variations in social policy across OECD nations.

Appendix

TABLE A1.1 *Examples of societal values extracted*

Societal value	Input variables	
Religiosity	▶ God is important in my life ▶ Have confidence in churches	▶ I am a religious person ▶ How often do you attend religious services
Conservative social norms[a]	▶ Justifiable: divorce ▶ Justifiable: abortion ▶ Justifiable: euthanasia	▶ Justifiable: prostitution ▶ Justifiable: homosexuality ▶ Justifiable: suicide
Permissive values on adherence to laws	▶ Justifiable: cheating on taxes ▶ Justifiable: claiming government benefits not entitled to	▶ Justifiable: someone accepting a bribe ▶ Justifiable: avoiding a fare on public transport
Optimistic values	▶ Feeling of happiness ▶ Satisfaction with your life	▶ How much freedom of choice and control in your life
Traditional family values[a]	▶ Marriage is an out-dated institution	▶ Approve of a single woman becoming a parent
Inter-personal tolerance[a]	▶ People that you would not like to have as neighbours: ▶ Drug addicts	▶ Heavy drinkers ▶ People with a criminal record ▶ Emotionally unstable people
Political activeness	▶ Political action: joining in boycotts ▶ Political action: attending lawful/peaceful demonstrations	▶ Political action: signing a petition ▶ Political action: joining unofficial strikes
Political orientedness	▶ Interest in politics	▶ How often discuss political matters with friends

Note: [a] Scores reversed.

Notes

1. See http://journals.cambridge.org/action/displayJournal?jid=JSP and http://scholar.google.com/scholar?oi=bibs&hl=en&q=pfau-effinger respectively
2. We should note that it has been argued that culture can help us to understand why and path-deviance occurs too (Jo, 2011; Pfau-Effinger, 2004a; van Oorschot, 2006: 24): for example, if societal values change.
3. To this end he approvingly cites the arguments of Wuthnow (1989), noting his 'subtle analysis of the comparative development of ideologies has elegantly shown how emerging worldviews, once they reach critical mass, can generate a set of culture-reproducing institutions, organizations, and specialized actors that greatly facilitate the spread and reproduction of that ideology' (Pierson, 2004: 39).
4. Even those offering what might be seen as a near deterministic approach offer suitable qualifications in this regard: Rieger and Liebfried (2003: 243), for instance, concede it is 'not culture per se that explains patterns in welfare state building'.
5. Whilst Hofstede applied a criterion of 0.5 in terms of the rank correlation coefficient (2001), we applied 0.7 (Jo, 2011) on the basis that with a small number of cases, the correlation coefficients may be comparatively higher.
6. Although all 11 factors show both unique and shared aspects of value-characteristics of society, some appeared to show more shared aspects than unique ones when inspected closely and were dropped in order to leave us with eight distinctive examples of societal values.
7. In most cases this was 2008, but in some cases missing values meant data for an earlier year had to be used for some factors for some cases. Primarily this was for non-European countries where specific questions had not been included in the national variant of the WVS.
8. We should also note that there are some missing values here that might add some noise to the analysis. Details of data coverage for each case can be found on the book's accompanying FigShare site.
9. For readers who are interested in exploring this further, we have placed plots for each example of a societal value, by welfare regime type, on our Fig Share site.

2
Exploring the Culture–Welfare Nexus: A Quantitative Comparative Analysis

Abstract: *In this chapter we report findings from a series of regression models exploring how far the cultural context helps us to understand cross-national variations in social policy making provision. Our models treat culture as one aspect of the context for social policy; while we include our examples of societal values as key independent variables in our regression models we also include indicators that aim to capture the economic, political and historical-institutional (welfare regime) context of policy making. Our quantitative analysis provides good support for the 'culture matters' thesis particularly when exploring 'old social risks'. However, we also note some limitations inherent in our approach, particularly when exploring 'new social risks', and point to the value of supplementing our regression analyses with complementary approaches.*

Keywords: culture; welfare state variations; societal values

Hudson, John, Nam Kyoung Jo and Antonia Keung. *Culture and the Politics of Welfare: Exploring Societal Values and Social Choices*. Basingstoke: Palgrave Macmillan, 2015. DOI: 10.1057/9781137457493.0007.

Exploring culture and welfare quantitatively

In this chapter we turn to the task of using our examples of societal values in quantitative empirical analyses of the impact of culture on welfare. We do some from a perspective cognisant with Pfau-Effinger's (2005; cf. 2004: 37–61) 'welfare culture approach' in which the impact of culture on welfare policy-making is mediated by political actors, social structures and institutions. We present a series of regression models that include independent variables related to each of these aspects (culture, politics, economy and institutions) in order to explain cross-national variations in key social policy provisions. Our examples of societal values extracted from European Values Study (EVS)/World Values Survey (WVS) data represent key independent variables in our models. They are supplemented by data on economic contexts (unemployment rate, female participation in the labour market rate, economic growth rate, gross domestic product [GDP] per capita) drawn from OECD datasets and the recently updated version of Kühner's (2007a, 2013) 'Comparative Welfare Reform Dataset' which is based on authoritative sources (OECD and International Monetary Fund [IMF]). Data on the political context (party composition of government; trade union density) also comes from Kühner's 'Comparative Welfare Reform Dataset' based on the 'Comparative Political Data Set 1960–2010' compiled by Armingeon et al. (2008, 2012). Finally, to capture the historical-institutional policy context for policy making countries were grouped into welfare regime types on the basis of Esping-Andersen's key works (1990, 1999) and Arts and Gelissen's (2002) intensive review of welfare regime typologies.[1] The dependent variables for our analysis are drawn from two key sources: social expenditure data from the OECD's SOCX database and data on family policy structures from the OECD's *Family Policy Structures Database* (OECD, 2013a). While we have data on societal values for some 59 countries, data on policy characteristics only covers OECD countries, reducing our sample to between 20 and 21 countries in our regression models.[2] To explore the influence of the cultural context on welfare we utilise proxies for policy decisions as our dependent variables. Firstly, replicating some of the analysis undertaken in our earlier work (Jo, 2011), we examine policy supports for the unemployed. Exploration of this area is at the core of much of the comparative welfare state literature, not least because it captures well what Esping-Andersen (1990) refers to as the extent to which welfare decommodifies labour: that is, the extent to which social policy provision protects citizens from the commodifying effects of capitalism by offering them income that is independent from their ability to sell their labour in the market. As such, it offers us a useful proxy for social rights generally and, indeed, for this reason the strength of support for the unemployed was one of the elements included in the decommodification index that was at the core of Esping-Andersen's ground breaking *Three Worlds of Welfare* analysis (Esping-Andersen, 1990).

However, as early critics of Esping-Andersen's work noted, while a focus on unemployment policy might capture the work-welfare nexus well, it does not speak to the care–welfare nexus that is also central to the overall shape of welfare regimes (Bleses and Seeleib-Kaiser, 2004; Ferragina, Seeleib-Kaiser and Tomlinson, 2013; Lewis, 1992). Esping-Andersen (1999) acknowledged this limitation in later work, constructing a defamilialisation index that captures the extent to which social policy promotes independence from family support and caring roles. Consequently, our second set of models focus on family policy in order to capture the care–welfare nexus. Significantly, this also allows us to include an area of policy in which there has been significant policy change over recent decades (Ferragina, Seeleib-Kaiser and Tomlinson, 2013). Indeed, following Taylor-Gooby (2004a, 2004b), we might usefully label our two policy areas as representing the 'old' social risks at the core of the traditional industrial welfare state and the 'new' social risks that are an increasingly prominent focus as high-income countries move away from male-breadwinner industrial economies towards post-industrial knowledge–based economies with high levels of female participation in the labour market.

We should note at the outset that we face some not insignificant methodological constraints in our task. Chief among these, arguably, is that the overall number of cases in our models is rather modest. While this is far from unusual in macro-level comparative welfare state research, it does nonetheless restrict the number of independent variables we can sensibly include in our models, particularly given that we have eight examples of societal values along with a range of variables relating to economic, political and social dimensions. Consequently, for each of our models we have constrained the number of independent variables included using a three-step process. While we detail the actual selection of indicators for each set of models in the sections that follow, it is worth outlining the general process here before we do so. First, we manually inspected descriptive statistics and simple charts that facilitated simple exploration of the relationship between each dependent variable and the proposed independent variables, allowing us to divide the latter into strong, medium and weak candidates for inclusion in our regression models, with the latter group dropped; secondly, our *prima facie* conclusions were tested through correlation analyses, with further adjustments made at this stage if necessary; finally, the candidate variables were matched against a priori theoretical assumptions about which variables ought to be included and final adjustments made here if necessary.

The cultural context and unemployment expenditure

Turning first to the 'old' social risks represented by unemployment policy, we use two different dependent variables that capture unemployment expenditure, one based on the percentage of GDP commanded by this area of activity (our primary measure) and the other based on the share of total social expenditure allocated to it. While the latter provides us with an effective indicator for exploring where unemployment expenditure fits in the balance of welfare state priorities, it has the potential to be misleading insofar as it tells us nothing about the overall level of welfare state effort for which an examination of the percentage of GDP allocated to unemployment spending is necessary.

In order to select the independent variables for our analysis we followed the procedure outlined above. After conducting a graphical examination through scatter plotting of the pooled data, data for each time point and data for each country,[3] the following were identified as strong candidates for inclusion:

- the unemployment rate (+) appeared to be the most likely influential factor, showing a positive relationship with our primary measure of unemployment policy in the pooled data, for each time point and for each country data (bar a few exceptions in the latter).
- GDP per capita (–), union density (+), interpersonal tolerance (+), and conservative social norms (–) also appeared likely to be influential as they showed the same pattern in the pooled data, for each time point and in many countries.

In addition, the following were identified as possibly influential:

- *Traditional family values* (–) and *optimistic values* (+). These variables showed the same pattern in the pooled data and for each time point, but in many countries the relationship pointed in the opposite direction

Other candidate variables were not expected to have a significant and constant impact on unemployment spending based on inspection of the raw data (GDP growth rate, cabinet composition, religiosity, permissive values on adherence to laws, Political activeness and political orientedness) and were removed from our analysis except for cabinet composition, which remained in on the basis of a priori theoretical assumptions. Key studies in the comparative welfare state literature have suggested that there is a partisan effect on welfare spending, with left-leaning governments more likely to be pro-welfare in their policy decisions (e.g., Castles, 1982; Hibbs, 1977). Though important contributions to the literature have suggested that partisan effects have weakened since the end of the era of welfare expansion (e.g., Huber and Stephens, 2001) we retain this variable given there is on-going debate. Finally, the welfare regime variables have to be included as they are our sole measure of the historical-institutional context, but for completeness we conducted a similar inspection of this data, which suggested that some impacts should be evident, albeit with variations across different regime types.

As a result of the above, *nine variables* were selected as candidates for our unemployment policy regression models: two economic contextual factors (unemployment rate, GDP per capita); two political contextual factors (union density; cabinet composition); one historical-institutional contextual factor (welfare regime); and, four cultural contextual factors (tolerance, conservative social norms, family values, optimistic values). Correlation analysis was undertaken to confirm these decisions (see Table 2.1); while this suggested that we might drop GDP per capita as a measure we retained this on the basis that having two separate measures of economic context might be useful, particularly given that unemployment (unsurprisingly) appears a key driver of unemployment spending.

Table 2.2 presents the results of our Ordinary Least Squares (OLS) regression models with unemployment expenditure as a percentage of GDP as the dependent variable. As expected, the unemployment rate drives a good deal of the variation in this field, with higher levels of unemployment clearly linked to higher levels of unemployment expenditure as a percentage GDP, underlining the (at least partially) cyclical nature of expenditure in this area. GDP per capita shows no significant influence until we add all other contexts into our model, when it shows

TABLE 2.1   Correlations with social expenditure on unemployment (as % GDP)

		N			N
Economic context					
Unemployment rate	0.519**	77	GDP per capita	−0.173	80
GDP growth rate	−0.089	80			
Political context					
Cabinet composition	0.157	80	Union density	0.445**	77
Cultural context					
Interpersonal tolerance	0.430**	77	Conservative social norms	−0.319**	99
Traditional family values	−0.266**	100	Optimistic values	0.253*	96
Religiosity	−0.174	98	Permissive values on adherence to laws	−0.035	89
Political activeness	0.109	100	Political orientedness	−0.127	91

** 0.05 level; *0.1 level.
Note: Historical-Institutional contextual factors (regime variables) are not examined here as they are purely categorical variables.

a negative significant association. Ostensibly this indicates that societies will allocate less of their overall resource to this area of policy as their economies become larger; it may be that this is capturing the changing dynamic of policy in this area over time, with the trend across the OECD generally being one of incremental reduction in the level of spending from the early 1990s until the mid-2000s, with particularly marked reductions in most of the countries that were high spenders in the 1980s (e.g., Denmark, the Netherlands, Sweden).[4]

Crucially, our earlier finding (Jo, 2011: 13–14) that the cultural context matters too is confirmed: we find that the predictive capacity of our model is clearly improved when the cultural context is added. Beyond this headline finding, some of the more detailed findings with respect to societal values merit reflection too.

Firstly, Table 2.2 shows that conservative social norms appear to have a significant negative association with the share of GDP allocated to unemployment spending. This makes sense insofar as we might reasonably expect more pejoratively judgemental attitudes towards the unemployed in societies where conservative social norms are stronger. Cross-national

TABLE 2.2 *Prediction of social expenditure on unemployment as % GDP (OLS)*

Model	1	2	3	4
Economic context				
GDP per capita	−0.004 (0.107)	−0.021 (0.098)	−0.111 (0.084)	−0.285 (0.078)***
Unemployment rate	0.134 (0.037)***	0.136 (0.034)***	0.166 (0.031)***	0.175 (0.026)***
Political context				
Cabinet composition index		0.039 (0.082)	0.076 (0.079)	0.022 (0.064)
Union density		0.019 (0.006)***	0.015 (0.006)**	0.018 (0.005)***
Historical-Institutional context (welfare regime, ref: Liberal)				
Conservative/Corporatist			0.684 (0.231)***	0.831 (0.261)***
Social Democratic			0.301 (0.315)	0.048 (0.326)
Southern European			−0.594 (0.283)**	0.366 (0.370)
Cultural context				
Interpersonal tolerance				0.347 (0.294)
Conservative social norms				−0.569 (0.328)*
Traditional family values				−0.740 (0.498)
Optimistic values				2.158 (0.604)***
R-square (adjusted values)	0.240 (0.209)	0.386 (0.335)	0.599 (0.537)	0.776 (0.716)
Model F-value	7.877***	7.547***	9.602***	12.944***
Number of cases			53	

*** 0.01 level; ** 0.05 level; * 0.1 level.

studies of public opinion data have more commonly explored this question from what might be seen as the reverse perspective, asking whether strong social solidarity (e.g., van Oorschot, 2000, 2008) or more egalitarian values (e.g., Blekesaune and Quadango, 2003) lead to higher social spending for the unemployed. Indeed, these key studies have suggested that they do: for example, Blekesaune and Quadango (2003: 422) found that public support for welfare policies towards the old was significantly correlated with the degree of egalitarianism in a nation. Arguably our conservative social norms societal value operates in a similar spectrum to social solidaristic or egalitarian values, but capturing the degree to which some groups are 'othered' through entrenched social norms. We would expect that the influence of this societal value on public opinion to feed through into policy decisions if our model of policy making advanced in Chapter 1 holds true and our regression model provides support for this hypothesis.

Secondly, Table 2.2 shows optimistic values to be positively associated with unemployment spending. This societal value comprises responses to questions about: how much freedom of choice and control there is in life; feelings of happiness; and, satisfaction with life. That this societal value has a significant positive association with unemployment spending echoes findings in our previous study (Jo, 2011); we argued there that it is difficult to explain why this should be so. Indeed, it is not unreasonable to assume that where people feel they have more control over their lives that the state might be expected to provide less support and so the association should point in the opposite directions. However, it might equally be surmised that people are more likely to feel in control of their lives – and show high levels of subjective well-being – if they are more strongly protected against economic risks by the state (i.e., this may reflect welfare provision feeding back into optimistic values or, at least, an iterative relationship between the two). Indeed, some theorists have suggested that the high levels of subjective well-being found in Nordic countries are connected with their strong social rights: Marklund (2013: 17) notes that 'the Nordic countries have scored well in comparative statistics on SWB [subjective well-being ... and] the Nordic model of welfare, with its focus upon collective and universal social security, has typically been seen as a key factor for these favourable results'. Similar observations about the links between high subjective well-being and high welfare spending – and the key role of Nordic countries in driving such associations in quantitative analyses – are made by Rothstein (2010). Beyond this, however, we might also point to the more theoretically rooted arguments of Berlant (2011) who, in her book *Cruel Optimism*, suggests that expansion of the state in key areas of social and economic policy 'motored' much of post-War optimism in Europe and America, but that the 'retraction, during the last three decades, of the social democratic promise' of this era (p. 12) has contributed to an 'attrition of a fantasy, a collectively invested form of life, the good life' (p. 26). Might it be that our models are pointing towards this thesis in some loose manner, with a 'post-War' sense of 'optimism' and the 'social democratic' model (or the overall decline thereof) in some way connected? We will explore this question in more detail in Chapter 4.

Our remaining societal values variables do not show significant associations with the overall level of unemployment spending, though it is worth noting that the effects point in the expected direction and hence we offer some tentative reflections here. Tolerance showed a positive (and significant) influence in our earlier work (Jo, 2011) and, given that the interpersonal tolerance factor in many ways captures the strength of social liberalism in a similar way that conservative social norms captures social illiberalism we might reasonably expect this to be so. Why, then, is there no clear influence this time? It may be that interpersonal tolerance is no longer significant in our latest models because: (i) our extracted examples of societal values inevitably are at best partial and overlapping dimensions of real societal values, (ii) that interpersonal tolerance and conservative social norms are two sides of an at least similar coin and (iii) that while our models struggle to pin down the specifics, on balance these results suggest that increased social liberalism fosters increased social spending on the unemployed and that the reverse is true also. Our remaining societal value is traditional family values and Table 2.2 shows a negative but not significant association, which is in line with our earlier findings (Jo, 2011). Given the repeated absence of a significant association we should perhaps not dwell on the potential link here too long, though the multi-level models computed as a robustness check did flag a significant negative association here. It could be hypothesised that in countries where traditional family values are stronger we might expect the role of the family in income protection to be stressed over the role of the state.

Interestingly, if we examine the impact of welfare regimes we can see (compared with the Liberal regime) the Southern European regime having a significant negative association until our societal values are added into the model, at which point this regime no longer has a significant association and the direction shifts from negative to positive. Given that both conservative social norms and traditional family values are strong in this regime it may be that our models struggle to disentangle the impacts of these multiple, perhaps overlapping, factors; we will return to this issue in Chapter 3. We can see a strong – and significant – positive influence of Conservative/Corporatist regime membership, which perhaps reflects the impact of the typically Bismarckian model of unemployment insurance in this regime whereby contributory schemes produce relatively generous earnings-related benefits (Esping-Andersen, 1990), though we should note that these schemes have faced increased pressure for reform in recent years (Palier, 2010). It is perhaps surprising that the Social Democratic regime does not show a significant positive association given the strong social rights associated with this regime; this could be because more recent changes to unemployment support in this regime have weakened the strength of social protections for the unemployed – this would chime with some parts of the analysis undertaken by Ferragina et al. (2013: 794) which suggests some Social Democratic nations have shifted away from the traditional model in this area – but it may also reflect that trade union density (which shows a positive and significant association with unemployment spending) is generally higher in this regime and that our models cannot easily disentangle the effects of the two. Finally, we should note that cabinet composition does not have a significant association with spending and, moreover, the direction of influence varies across our models, perhaps lending support to claims that partisan effects have weakened over time.

Table 2.3 reports the findings using our alternative dependent variable: unemployment spending as a share of total social spending. This allows us to explore the relative priority – within welfare state budgets – attached to protecting the unemployed as opposed to overall level of finance allocated to it. The core findings are extremely similar, including that inclusion of the societal values improves the explanatory power of our models. The welfare regime and political contexts operate in largely the same manner, the level of unemployment continues to be a key driver and, with respect to societal values, we again see optimistic values being an important factor.[5] Conservative social norms no longer displays a significant association (though the direction remains the same), but traditional family values now shows a significant negative association. This is consistent with the tentative explanation we advanced above for

TABLE 2.3 Prediction of share of social expenditure on unemployment (OLS)

Model	1	2	3	4
Economic context				
GDP per capita	−0.209 (0.405)	−0.266 (0.376)	−0.521 (0.351)	−1.253 (0.329)***
Unemployment rate	0.617 (0.140)***	0.630 (0.130)***	0.733 (0.129)***	0.776 (0.110)***
Political context				
Cabinet composition index		−0.069 (0.315)	0.257 (0.332)	0.079 (0.269)
Union Density		0.067 (0.021)***	0.068 (0.024)***	0.065 (0.021)***
Historical-Institutional context (welfare regime, ref: Liberal)				
Conservative/Corporatist			1.071 (.964)	2.404 (1.094)**
Social Democratic			−0.742 (1.316)	−0.519 (1.367)
Southern European			−3.018 (1.180)**	1.333 (1.555)
Cultural context				
Interpersonal tolerance				0.618 (1.233)
Conservative social norms				−0.590 (1.377)
Traditional family values				−4.088 (2.088)*
Optimistic values				10.663 (2.534)***
R-square (adjusted values)	0.338 (0.312)	0.454 (0.409)	0.578 (0.512)	0.762 (0.698)
Model F-value	12.784***	9.981***	8.798***	11.951***
Number of cases			53	

*** 0.01 level; ** 0.05 level; * 0.1 level.

this societal value – that in countries where traditional family values are stronger we might expect the role of the family in income protection to be stressed over the role of the state – but, crucially, given that this model deals with the *share* of welfare spending allocated to the unemployed rather than the overall level of spending we can extend this hypothesis a stage further by suggesting the effect of traditional family values ought to be stronger here (than when examining overall spending as % GDP) because we should expect (the generally smaller) welfare state budgets in countries with strong traditional family values to display a greater emphasis on welfare provisions that are more clearly outwith the scope of budgetary redistribution within the family. So, for example, we might expect expenditure on items such as health care to form a larger share of the total social budget and cash transfers a smaller amount.

In summary, our regression models provide strong support for the 'culture matters' thesis when exploring unemployment policy. The explanatory power of our models improved by inclusion of the societal values data and we are able to detect statistically significant influences for some our examples of societal values that are largely consistent with findings from previous work and suggestions made by key comparative welfare state theorists. Indeed, we might even argue that the cultural influences show through more clearly – and more consistently in terms of matching key theoretical suggestions – than is the case for our political or historical-institutional contexts.

The cultural context and family policy expenditure

Normative debates about 'who should get what and why' are expected to particularly show the impact of societal values on decision making where normative issues are prominent in political discourse (Jo, 2011: 7; see also van Oorschot, 2000). We chose to examine unemployment expenditure because debates around support for the unemployed have been amongst the most contentious in recent years. There are good reasons to extend our analysis to embrace different policy decisions, not least because different values ought to impact on different policy debates, and we repeat our approach here with an examination of family policy expenditures. This allows us to compare the impact of the cultural context in a policy area firmly associated with traditional social risks, the industrial welfare state and class-based political conflict (i.e., unemployment policy), with one at the centre of debates about the new social risks addressed by the post-industrial welfare state and perhaps tied to a new form of welfare politics (Taylor-Gooby, 2004a). We again examine spending as a percentage of GDP and as a share of total social expenditure.

As with our analysis of unemployment policy, we began by narrowing down our independent variables using the procedure outlined at the start of the chapter. After conducting a graphical examination through scatter plotting of the pooled data, data for each time point and data for each country, the following were identified as strong candidates for inclusion:

▸ Female labour participation rate (+), religiosity (–), conservative social norms (–), GDP per capita (–), and welfare regime (though with varying impacts across types): they each show the same pattern in the pooled data, data for each time point data and in many countries.

In addition, the following were identified as possibly influential:

▸ Unemployment rate (–), cabinet composition (+), union density (+), interpersonal tolerance (+), traditional family values (–), optimistic values (+) and political orientedness (+). They showed the same pattern in the pooled and each time point data, but the relationships were very weak and in many (around the half) of the countries the relationship was in the opposite direction. In some respects, it might just mean that these factors have no strong impact.

Other candidate variables were not expected to have a significant and constant impact on spending based on inspection of the raw data – GDP growth rate, permissive values on adherence to laws, and political activeness – and removed from our analysis except for cabinet composition, which remained in on the basis of a priori theoretical assumptions.

Based on the above, we could select just the 5 variables that are strong candidates, the 12 that are strong and possibly influential, or the 5 strong candidates supplemented with a smaller number of others based on a priori theoretically rooted assumptions and the results of correlation analysis. We adopted the latter on the basis that 5 is a modest number of independent variables but 12 is too many. Assisted by our correlation analysis (Table 2.4) we selected female labour participation rate and GDP per capita for the economic context. We stuck with both cabinet composition and union density for the political context; although our a

TABLE 2.4   Correlations with social expenditure on family (as % GDP)

		N			N
Economic context					
GDP per capita	0.286***	81	GDP growth rate	−0.087	81
Unemployment rate	−0.198*	77	Female labour participation rate	0.344***	65
Political context					
Cabinet composition	0.325***	81	Union density	0.333***	78
Cultural context					
Religiosity	−0.523***	104	Conservative social norms	−0.550***	105
Interpersonal tolerance	0.284***	82	Traditional family values	−0.258***	104
Optimistic values	0.281***	103	Permissive values on adherence to laws	−0.129	95
Political activeness	0.366***	107	Political orientedness	0.277***	96

*** 0.01 level; ** 0.05 level; *0.1 level.
Note: Historical-Institutional contextual factors (regime variables) are not examined here as they are purely categorical variables.

priori theoretical assumption is that trade union density is less likely to be linked to this area of policy than cabinet composition,[6] the two show a similar correlation. Finally, religiosity and conservative social norms perform as expected, showing the strongest correlation so remained in our selection. Of the remaining societal values, most show the same modest strength of correlation; given this we selected traditional family values as our final variable on the basis of a priori assumptions that family values ought to have an impact on family policy. Along with the regime variable this provided us with a total of eight independent variables, just one fewer than in our models for unemployment expenditure.

Table 2.5 presents the results of our regression models with family policy expenditure as a percentage of GDP as the dependent variable. Though the inclusion of cultural contexts improves the model, it does so much more modestly than in our unemployment expenditure models and so the model provides much less clear support for the culture matters thesis. Moreover, only one of our societal values shows a significant association with spending – religiosity – with a negative association being flagged. Esping-Andersen's (1990: 27 and 112) original conceptualisation of his three welfare regimes acknowledged that religion ought to play a key role in shaping cross-national policy difference, with a particular

TABLE 2.5 Prediction of social expenditure on family policy as % GDP (OLS)

Model	1	2	3	4
Economic context				
GDP per capita	0.207 (0.116)*	0.227 (0.099)**	0.158 (0.078)**	0.195 (0.081)**
Female participation rate	0.033 (0.016)**	0.034 (0.014)**	-0.010 (0.017)	-0.012 (.017)
Political context				
Cabinet composition index		0.272 (.088)***	0.241 (0.077)***	0.156 (0.077)**
Union density		0.022 (0.006)***	0.005 (0.006)	0.011 (0.006)*
Historical-Institutional context (welfare regime, ref: Liberal)				
Conservative/Corporatist			0.355 (0.256)	0.157 (0.287)
Social Democratic			1.072 (0.338)***	0.654 (0.376)*
Southern European			-1.203 (0.330)***	-0.807 (0.358)**
Cultural context				
Religiosity				-1.157 (0.374)***
Conservative social norms				0.242 (0.417)
Traditional family values				0.438 (0.505)
R-square (adjusted values)	0.159 (0.128)	0.409 (0.363)	0.681 (0.635)	0.740 (0.683)
Model F-value	5.097***	8.995***	14.920***	13.081***
Number of cases			57	

*** 0.01 level; ** 0.05 level; * 0.1 level.

nod towards the role of the Church in limiting the extent of family policy in the Conservative/Corporatist regime.[7] However, it is puzzling that while religiosity shows the negative association with family spending this suggests, we find no significantly negative association between spending and membership of the Conservative/Corporatist regime; in fact, our model displays a positive but insignificant one. This may be because the regression model cannot disentangle interactions between religiosity and membership of this type. In a similar vein, the direction of conservative social norms and traditional family values in the regression model is the reverse from that in the bivariate correlations in Table 2.4: this might again be because the models cannot easily disentangle complex interactions between the societal values and some of the regime types. We explore this issue more in Chapter 3, but overall these issues mean that our model provides modest support for the culture matters thesis with respect to the overall level of family policy spending.

Indeed, the most influential factors seem drawn from outside of the cultural context. We have already noted that our model does not capture a clear regime effect for the Conservative/Corporatist type, but elsewhere we do see some clear regime effects and, on the whole, we might argue that they appear to outweigh the cultural factors. Compared to the Liberal regime, Social Democratic regime members are likely to have higher levels of family policy spending which is to be expected given Esping-Andersen's (1999) suggestion that defamilialisation patterns map onto decommodification patterns. By contrast, membership of the Southern European regime, which Esping-Andersen did not include as a separate cluster in his work, is significantly associated with lower spending still than the Liberal regime. This fits with key theoretical works identifying this cluster, which suggest that a key feature of this ideal type is the limited degree of state penetration in the provision of welfare (Ferrera, 1996).

In terms of political and economic factors, Table 2.5 shows cabinet composition is positively and significantly associated with the level of spending on family policy. This is particularly interesting given the weak link it displayed with unemployment spending. It is, perhaps, also consistent with the developmental theory of realignment (Giger, 2009; Inglehart and Norris, 2000, 2003) which suggests that women have shifted from being more right leaning than men in their voting preferences to being more left leaning than men voting preferences as economies have moved from industrial to post-industrial structures, though we should be cautious in presuming both that left parties have responded by increasing support for family policy and that such an approach would be successful in attracting the votes of women (Manow and Emmenegger, 2012). Morgan (2009) notes that trade unions have adopted varying responses to promoting/blocking expansion of childcare across Europe historically, so it interesting to note the a (weakly) significant positive association is shown here. Finally, our model shows that GDP per capita is positively and significantly associated with the overall level of family policy spending, reflecting that there has been strong growth in this area of policy in more recent years; it is unlikely there is a 'causal' link here and that, instead, this merely reflects the rise of 'new' social risk agendas as economies have become more post-industrial.

Our second model, which explores the share of social spending allocated to family policy (Table 2.6), shows remarkably similar findings: the influence (and significance) of our economic, political and institutional factors remains very much the same.[8] Inclusion of the societal values again improves the explanatory power of the model, but only modestly so and religiosity remains significantly negatively associated with spending. Though not showing a significant association in either case, conservative social norms and traditional family values again show a positive association. These consistent patterns are, perhaps, worth flagging as curious despite the lack of statistical significance: as we note above, in bivariate analysis the variables show a clear negative association with the level of spending, so it may be that there are complex interactions between welfare regimes and societal values operating here. For instance, in regimes where state intervention is more common, conservative social norms may facilitate an expansion of state spending on (say) cash benefits that support the traditional nuclear family, but in regimes where state intervention is typically eschewed they may serve to further constrain state spending. Indeed, a good deal of comparative work exploring gender in the welfare state has noted that seemingly common (e.g., feminist) political movements have produced divergent policy outcomes across countries with respect to policies targeted at families with children (e.g.,Myles and Quadango, 2002: 48; Orloff, 1996).

All told, however, these are rather modest findings and at first sight an examination of family policy spending appears to provide less strong support for the culture matters thesis than our analysis of unemployment expenditure. That said, it might be argued that while the exploration of unemployment expenditure has a clear link to an identifiable

TABLE 2.6 Prediction of share of social expenditure on family policy (OLS)

Model	1	2	3	4
Economic context				
GDP per capita	0.963 (0.464)**	1.015 (0.419)**	0.860 (0.382)**	1.159 (0.384)***
Female participation rate	0.126 (0.064)*	0.131 (0.058)**	-0.046 (0.084)	-0.039 (0.081)
Political context				
Cabinet composition index		0.720 (0.369)*	1.047 (0.376)***	0.604 (0.364)
Union density		0.084 (0.025)***	0.050 (0.030)*	0.084 (0.029)***
Historical-Institutional context (welfare regime, ref: Liberal)				
Conservative/Corporatist			-1.530 (1.246)	-2.148 (1.360)
Social Democratic			0.171 (1.648)	-1.839 (1.778)
Southern European			-6.456 (1.607)***	-4.021 (1.691)**
Cultural context				
Religiosity				-6.384 (1.769)***
Conservative social norms				2.011 (1.972)
Traditional family values				3.296 (2.389)
R-square (adjusted values)	0.175 (0.145)	0.356 (0.307)	0.533 (0.466)	0.642 (0.564)
Model F-value	5.734***	7.188***	7.994***	8.237***
Number of cases			57	

*** 0.01 level; ** 0.05 level; * 0.1 level.

and relatively coherent policy area, this is less true for family spending. Indeed, the OECD expenditure data for this area conflates spending on very different policies such as universal child benefits, in-work supplements for families with children and supplementary payments to households that might include items such as income top-ups for lone parent families or large families. It also includes expenditure on day care services and home help. In other words, a broad range of policies falls under this heading. If our goal is to focus on the deeply normative debates about 'who should get what and why' (Jo, 2011: 7; see also van Oorschot, 2000) then family policy expenditure may lack some suitability as a proxy for competing value laden policy choices, not just because it covers a broad range of policy areas, but also because it tells us nothing about some key value laden choices such as whether cash benefits for families with children provide extra support for lone parent families (on the basis of their increased risk of poverty) or reduced support for them (on the basis that traditional two parent households are 'penalised' if policy favours lone parents). Indeed, there is a long-standing critique of comparative analyses that use aggregated expenditure-based dependent variables (for an overview see Clasen and Siegel, 2008; Kühner, 2007b). What matters more for such critics are the details of programme structures and rules: can an examination based in such an approach provide clearer support for the culture matters thesis in the area of family policy?

To explore this, we offer a final regression model below that makes use of data on family policy structures using a dependent variable relating to maternity leave policy structures: the full-time equivalent rate that multiplies the length of leave by the replacement rate. However, we should note that our data set only covers 1996–2009 so we trade-off selecting a more focused dependent variable for a smaller number of cases.[9] The results are presented in Table 2.7. In terms of the core 'culture matters' thesis, we still find only modest support for it when examining programme structures rather than spending, with the explanatory power of the model increasing only marginally once our societal values are included, though more of our societal values are significant in this model. Religiosity continues to have a clearly negative association with the generosity of provision. The direction of conservative social norms points in the same direction as for our spending data and is now significantly association with the policy outcome; this further deepens the puzzle noted above, suggesting that either the welfare regime-societal value interactions are very complex (and so masking the true influence

TABLE 2.7 Prediction the generosity of maternity leave FTE rates (OLS)

Model	1	2	3	4
Economic context				
GDP per capita	−1.072 (1.438)	0.029 (1.242)	0.077 (1.027)	0.402 (1.037)
Female participation rate	0.241 (0.206)	0.254 (0.173)	−0.194 (0.224)	−0.089 (0.222)
Political context				
Cabinet composition index		4.488 (1.116)***	3.360 (0.923)***	2.827 (1.072)**
Union density		0.046 (0.070)	−0.181 (0.076)**	−0.188 (0.090)**
Historical-Institutional context (welfare regime, ref: Liberal)				
Conservative/Corporatist			2.166 (3.237)	3.979 (3.714)
Social Democratic			19.303 (4.007)***	22.053 (5.956)***
Southern European			−0.430 (4.314)	2.736 (4.907)
Cultural context				
Religiosity				−9.615 (5.408)*
Conservative social norms				11.239 (6.288)*
Traditional family values				4.906 (7.306)
R-square (adjusted values)	0.044 (−0.010)	0.367 (0.290)	0.643 (0.560)	0.703 (0.593)
Model F-value	0.814	4.783***	7.732***	6.398***
Number of cases			38	

*** 0.01 level; ** 0.05 level; * 0.1 level.

of this societal value) or it may be highlighting that conservative social norms do in fact play a role in supporting policies that are seen to be 'pro-family'; we explore this issue more in the next chapter. Traditional family values does not show a significant association.

In terms of the other factors, the significant role of left parties in supporting more generous support continues to show in this model and the enhanced level of support in Social Democratic regime members is more clearly pronounced when we examine programme structures rather than spending data, while trade union density shows a significant negative association, perhaps hinting at the conflicting strategies they have adopted across countries. Interestingly, economic growth is not a significant factor, perhaps reflecting that reforms to these supports tend to take place in a slow and incremental manner that is not sensitive to short-term changes; the direction of influence is positive, perhaps reflecting that some countries expanded support during the relatively strong growth years of the early-to-mid 2000s.

As with the exploration of expenditure data, we must acknowledge some limits in looking very closely at specific policy structures. Capturing policy decisions via programme rules makes sense only if we can meaningfully represent the underlying values of those decisions with simple indicators. Our programme rules data is by no means perfect: for instance, the USA scores 0 in each element of our maternity policy structures data but these scores mask the fact that there are at least partially functioning schemes in place. We should also acknowledge that support comes in the form of packages of complimentary benefits with entitlements varying on the basis of household composition and income (cf. Bradshaw and Finch, 2002), so capturing programme structures in a single indicator requires a good degree of simplification of the complex reality. As such, we have some sympathy for Castles' (2002) suggestion that OECD SOCX expenditure data still provides a useful proxy for welfare state effort in most instances.

To summarise our exploration of family policy spending and structures, our regression models provide at best lukewarm support for culture matters thesis. However, it should be stressed that our models do not provide clear evidence *against* the culture matters thesis. Indeed, when interpreting findings we find plenty of hints that culture *may* matter and, as we reflect above, it may be that our models struggle to disentangle the intertwined influences of welfare regime, cultural context and politics. Partly this may be because there is greater dynamism in the area of family policy than in most other areas of social policy, with significant and in some cases quite fundamental expansions of state activity having occurred since the 1980s (Ferragina, Seeleib-Kaiser and Tomlinson, 2013). This, in turn, creates analytic challenges and may require us to adopt less common methods that are better able to handle 'spiky' distributions of data (Ferragina, Seeleib-Kaiser and Tomlinson, 2013). We turn to the question of whether alternative methods can help us tease out the ways in which societal values are shaping family policy below and in the next chapter.

Conclusion

There are limitations in our approach that must be accounted for when interpreting our findings. These naturally include limits in the measures chosen, not just our use of our examples of societal values as a proxy for culture, but limitations in our other variables too. Indeed, our analysis of family policies in particular has demonstrated the on-going relevance of 'dependent variable problem' debate (Kühner, 2007b). Beyond this, we should acknowledge that viewing culture as a series of societal values treated as independent variables means we cannot easily capture what might be important interactions between them and other variables such as the welfare regimes. Though we have analysed a large amount of data here, the limited number of observations in our models prevents us from undertaking more complex regression analyses that might capture some of these interactions: for instance, we cannot include interaction terms for key independent variables.

Nonetheless, the results presented here add value to the culture and welfare debate. In particular, we have shown that the in-between conception of culture offers a fruitful avenue for exploring the impact of the cultural context on social policy making. We have exposed our analytic framework to tougher tests than in our earlier work, using data covering a longer time period, more countries and a broader range of policy areas. In so doing, we believe that we have provided strong empirical evidence to support the 'culture matters' in welfare policy making thesis with regard to old social risks and some more qualified support with regard to new social risks represented.

As future waves of EVS/WVS are released and more data on policy inputs is collected, some of the limitations we note will be slowly overcome. In the meantime, some of the key hypotheses advanced above concerning the impacts of specific societal values on policy might usefully be explored via detailed country case studies and/or using configurational comparative methods (Rihoux and Ragin, 2008) that are better placed to draw out complex interactions with modestly sized data sets. It is to this task we now turn in Chapters 3 and 4.

Chapter summary

This chapter makes three key points:

- Using our examples of societal values as a proxy for culture in regression models we can provide strong evidence for the 'culture matters' thesis with respect to old social risks represented by unemployment spending. Our models suggest that optimistic values are positively associated with higher levels of overall spending on the unemployed, while the converse was true for conservative social norms.
- The same approaches provide less strong support for the culture matters thesis when we explore new social risks represented by family policy spending. There was fairly strong evidence to suggest that higher levels of religiosity are linked to less extensive family policy provision. However, historical-institutional and political factors appear more clearly influential in this area of policy, with membership of the Social Democratic regime and a left-wing government providing the most favourable environment(s) for expansive family policy.
- Despite the methodological advances outlined here, our models struggled to capture some of the complex interactions between culture and welfare regimes though they pointed to many ways in which culture *might* be influential in shaping social policy, particularly for family policy. We suspect the influence of conservative social norms and traditional family values are not being detected in this area because of interactions with welfare regimes. Supplementing our regression models with configurational methods may help us to dig deeper.

Notes

1. Liberal: Australia, Canada, Ireland, New Zealand, Switzerland, United Kingdom and the United States; conservative/corporatist: Austria, Belgium, France, Germany, Luxembourg and the Netherlands; Social Democratic: Denmark, Finland, Norway and Sweden; and Southern European: Greece, Italy, Portugal and Spain.
2. Having data for up to four time points for each country usefully adds additional cases to our models but also creates the possibility that the values of a variable at different time points from a particular country might be associated with each other and so violate regression assumptions. Multilevel models (MLM) are able to handle hierarchical nested data by allowing the intercept and/or slope to vary from country to country but bring their own methodological challenges particularly for work based on relatively small samples (Tabachnick and Fidell, 2007; Twisk, 2006). We therefore supplement standard OLS models with multi-level models able to identify patterns of nested data: we report the OLS models in the text here in the main, but use our MLM findings act as a sensitivity analysis, noting in the footnotes when these deviate. With regards to the temporal dimension of our models it is important to note (as detailed in Chapter 1) that data for our societal values is not available on annual basis. Rather than matching our variables to individual years covered by the EVS/WVS data we chose to use five-year averages in order to minimise the impact of any exceptional and unrepresentative scores in the independent or dependent variables (e.g., a short lived government from outside the political mainstream or a very temporary rise in unemployment).
3. The charts can be inspected on our FigShare site.
4. Plots for each variable, by country and over time, can be found on our FigShare site.
5. Our fixed effects multi-level model finds a positive but not significant association for the conservative/corporatist regime type.
6. We assume this partly because union membership tends to be higher within traditionally male dominated industrial sectors but also because union membership has tended to decline as economies have become post-industrial and it is the rise of the latter that key theorists have connected with the shift in focus towards new social risks (e.g., Taylor-Gooby, 2004b).
7. As he put it (Esping-Andersen, 1990: 27) the corporatist regimes are 'typically shaped by the Church, and hence strongly committed to the preservation of traditional familyhood. Social insurance typically excludes non-working wives, and family benefits encourage motherhood. Day care, and similar family services, are conspicuously underdeveloped; the principle of 'subsidiarity' serves to emphasise that the state will only interfere when the

family's capacity to service its members is exhausted'. Similarly, in constructing a quantitative model of welfare politics (Esping-Andersen, 1990: 112), he included measures capturing Catholic and Christian Democrat mobilisation based on the 'presupposition that where Catholicism is strong, the dominant ideals of social justice are likely to be coloured by the world-view of the Church [... so] the variable seeks to capture a general presence of the Catholic teachings on social policy'

8 The cabinet composition is no longer significant in our OLS model, but it remains so in our fixed effects multi-level model.
9 In other words, we pay a different price in terms of the overall robustness of our analysis. Given this shortened to frame, and in order to maximise the number of observations in our model, we therefore deviate from using five-year averages for the dependent variable for this stage of our analysis, instead using a four-year mean for 1996–1999 and five-year mean for 2004–2008.

3
Exploring the Culture–Welfare Nexus: A Qualitative Comparative Analysis

Abstract: *This chapter builds on the findings presented in Chapter 2, using fuzzy set Qualitative Comparative Analysis (fsQCA) to explore issues that our regression models struggled to disentangle. After reviewing some of the key aspects of the approach, we outline a three-step model of fsQCA that allows us to drill beneath the headline findings of some of our regression models. Focusing on the example of family policy expenditure we explore the ways in which societal values and welfare regimes appear to interact.*

Keywords: culture; fsQCA; societal values; welfare state models

Hudson, John, Nam Kyoung Jo and Antonia Keung. *Culture and the Politics of Welfare: Exploring Societal Values and Social Choices.* Basingstoke: Palgrave Macmillan, 2015. DOI: 10.1057/9781137457493.0008.

The limits to exploring culture and welfare quantitatively

In this chapter we aim to shed light on some of the issues our regression models struggled to explore, using a fuzzy set Qualitative Comparative Analysis (fsQCA) approach in order to do so. A full treatment of the principles of QCA is not possible here (see Ragin, 2000, 2008; Rihoux and Ragin, 2008), but given the method is likely to be unfamiliar to many readers we sketch some key features here at the outset. The method was initially designed for those undertaking cross-national work with a small number of cases (Hudson and Kühner, 2013; Ragin, 2000; Rihoux and Ragin, 2008) and is designed to act as a bridge between qualitative and quantitative approaches.[1]

The starting point of QCA is that cases (in our study, countries) are best understood as distinct configurations of multiple conceptually rooted dimensions. The approach requires researchers to specify the key conceptual dimensions that are the focus of analysis, each of which becomes a set in which cases can have varying degrees of membership (Ragin, 2000). In crisp set QCA (csQCA) cases are simply either members or non-members of a set, but in fsQCA membership is more 'fuzzy' and each case is placed between '0' (full non-membership) and '1' (full membership) for each set. Crucially, calibration of set membership need not (ideally: should not) be simply based on rescaling raw statistical data via arithmetic computation so the top and bottom cases are scored as 1 and 0 with others scaled between the two. Instead, QCA allows researchers to reconsider data from a conceptual viewpoint: for example, if a study included a set on 'high spending welfare states' it may be, following review of conceptual debates and based on case knowledge, that the researcher decides that spending in excess of 20% of GDP is high so all countries spending at or above this level score 1 (fully in the 'high spending welfare states' set). Table 3.1 outlines the most common approaches for calibrating sets (see Ragin, 2008).

Determining the scores for each set is central to QCA, but equally important is how multiple dimensions are combined. Here QCA relies on Boolean algebra and set logic (Ragin, 2008; Schneider and Wagemann, 2006), with two key principles utilised to analyse combinations of sets: the logical NOT (the negation principle) and the logical AND (the intersection or minimum principle). Together, these two principles can be used to calculate all possible combinations of the multiple sets being

TABLE 3.1 Creating scores for QCA sets

Crisp set	Four-value fuzzy set	Six-value fuzzy set	Continuous fuzzy set
1 = fully in the set	1 = fully in the set	1 = fully in the set	1 = fully in the set
		0.8 = mostly, but not fully in the set	More in than out of the set: $0.5 < X_i < 1$
	0.67 = more in than out of the set	0.6 = more or less in the set	
			0.5 = neither in nor out of the set
	0.33 = more out than in the set	0.4 = more or less out of the set	More out than in the set: $0 < X_i < 0.5$
		0.2 = mostly, but not fully out of the set	
0 = fully out of the set	0 = fully out of the set	0 = fully out of the set	0 = fully out of the set

Source: Adapted from Ragin, 2008.

analysed (the property space).[2] Two further key principles of QCA are particularly pertinent for exploring some of the unresolved issues we flagged at the end of Chapter 2. The first is *conjunctural causation*: that the impact of a condition may be contingent upon its combination with another condition. For example, traditional family values may not impact on policy decisions about family spending alone but will do so when combined with high levels of religiosity. The second is *equifinality*: that there may be different routes to the same outcome. For example, high levels of family spending may arise due to strong left wing governments OR strong Christian Democrat governments.[3] Proponents of fsQCA approaches argue that, even with interaction terms, regression models struggle to incorporate these principles and that fsQCA offers clear advantages here as consequence (Ragin, 2008). As Ragin puts it, in looking to explore the impact of combinations of factors on a particular outcome, QCA methods offer advantages over regression models because they see 'causal conditions not as adversaries in the struggle to explain variation in dependent variables, but as potential collaborators in the production of outcomes' (Ragin, 2008: 113).

Given that we flagged potentially hidden interactions between components as a limiting factor of our regression-based analysis of family policy, fsQCA approaches may well be able to help us dig deeper into the welfare–culture links in this area policy. Indeed, this is particularly so given that we struggled to see the influence of one of the societal values we would, based on a priori assumptions, expect to see playing a role: traditional family values. This gives us good reason to explore the potential for using fsQCA methods to supplement our regression models in this area.[4] However, while the case for using fsQCA here sounds compelling in principle, there are significant challenges in adapting the approach to 'match' our regression models. It is to these challenges that we now turn.

Methods

Overview of approach

Exponents of fsQCA argue that it is particularly suited to the analysis of how complex combinations of conditions might be linked to a particular outcome when the overall number of cases in a study is small or medium sized. However, one of the issues typically encountered when undertaking fsQCA is that of *limited diversity*. Because the approach proceeds on the analysis of all logically possible combinations of each set, consideration of even a relatively modest number of conditions can create a large property space. With a large number of sets, limited diversity means many possible combinations are unlikely to be populated by real world examples so remain purely hypothetical unobserved cases dubbed *logical remainders*. Our regression models for family policy had up to 9 independent variables, 12 if we count each welfare regime type separately, and these 12 factors provide a total 4,096 possible logical combinations across a maximum of 57 cases. Consequently, the number of logical remainders would be enormous were we to simply place all independent variables from our regression models into a single fsQCA model.

Schneider and Wagemann (2003, 2006) have suggested that some of the challenges arising from limited diversity can be dealt with using a two-step approach to fsQCA. As the name implies, in essence their approach involves breaking the analysis into two separate steps. In the first-step analysis focuses on remote or distant factors (defined as 'those characteristics of cases that do not change easily over time or that cannot change under any circumstances' – Schneider and Wagemann, 2003: 25),

TABLE 3.2   *Factors and outcomes in three-step fsQCA*

	Distant factors	Intermediate factors	Proximate factors
Conditions	Historical-institutional context (welfare regimes): ▸ Conservative / Corporatist ▸ Liberal ▸ Social Democratic ▸ Southern European	Cultural context (examples of societal values): ▸ Conservative social norms ▸ Religiosity ▸ Traditional family values	Political and economic contexts: ▸ Party composition of government ▸ Economic growth
Time	Assumed to be fixed	Long-term average, 1981–2008	5-year averages, time points circa 1981, 1990, 1999, 2008
Outcomes	Family policy spending (% GDP)	Family policy spending (% GDP)	Family policy spending (% GDP)
Time	Long-term average, 1981–2008	Long-term average, 1981–2008	5-year averages, time points circa 1981, 1990, 1999, 2008

reducing the number of factors (and so the number of combinations) in this stage. Then, in the second stage, the proximate or near factors (those that are faster moving and more changeable) are analysed but, crucially, separate analyses are conducted for each of the sub-groupings identified in the first stage of the analysis.[5]

Promising though this approach is for our purposes, we face challenges in deploying it within our theoretical framework for we have what might be seen as *three stages* operating at different speeds: historical-institutional contexts represented by *welfare regimes* (theorised as very slow moving remote factors); *political/economic contexts* (that seem to be good candidates for being treated as regularly changing proximate factors); and, *societal values* (that we theorise as being dynamically stable and so seem to fit in-between the two as *intermediate* factors). Rather than adapt our theoretical model outlined in Chapter 1 – whereby culture is believed to interact with historical-institutional, political and economic contexts – we instead modify Schneider and Wagemann's two-step model for our analysis here, creating a three-step fsQCA that examines remote, intermediate and then proximate factors. However, adapting the technique is by no means straightforward. A key challenge is that even adding a second step reduces the number of cases analysed together as we move from step 1 to step 2 because the sub-branches identified in step 1 are analysed separately. Adding a third step would often leave almost no cases in many instances as we move to the third step. To circumvent this we add a further consideration of the temporal dimension to our analytic strategy. Specifically, in steps 1 and 2 – which are based on the analysis of very slow moving *distant factors* and slow moving *intermediate factors* – we base our sets on data relating to long-term averages and treat each country in our sample as a single case. However, in step 3, when we examine faster changing *proximate* factors, we base our sets on medium term averages and include multiple time points for each country in our sample, treating each time point for each country as a separate case[6] (see Table 3.2). The goals of our approach here should be read as being deliberately modest: we are *not* aiming to reinvent fsQCA or claiming our approach establishes a new standard for such studies. Instead, we are merely adapting existing fsQCA approaches to fit with both our theoretical model of how culture might influence social policy making *and* the dependent and independent variables included in our regression models. Our ultimate goal here are to use an fsQCA approach to help us move from the rather abstract, data driven and variable centred analysis presented so far, towards a better understanding of the findings from this analysis by connecting us more closely with the cases themselves. As such, what we present here might best be viewed as an attempt to adapt existing fsQCA techniques to help us *map patterns within our cases*, identifying different branching effects in policy arising from the influence of different process, that is, the long-term historical-institutional influences, medium term cultural influences and shorter term economic and political influences. To this end, we keep technical information to a minimum in the core text, with more detail in the chapter appendix; the figures illustrating our findings contain some technical data that is explained in the chapter appendix.

Creating sets and identifying pathways

Our analysis explores whether or not countries are members of the 'high family policy spending' set. 'High' spending evidently a relative concept and we base membership (or non-membership) of it on the basis of long-term averages for family policy spending as a percentage of GDP. (Fuller details of the thresholds for this, and other, sets can be found in the chapter appendix.) This provides us with our outcome measure. The *distant factors* are merely the welfare regime type memberships for each case (Chapter 2). The *intermediate factors* comprise the three examples of societal values included in our regression models: conservative social norms; traditional family values; and, religiosity. Finally, in terms of the *proximate factors* we include one each for the political and economic contexts: the party composition of government and economic growth; we chose economic growth rather than GDP per capita for the economic context and cabinet composition rather the union density for the political context on the basis these factors are the most likely to fluctuate over the short term. Table 3.2 provides a summary of all sets included here.

As well as specifying how our sets are constructed, we also need to specify how the analysis will move from step to step. In principle this is straightforward: for each step of our analysis we simply aim to identify set relations analytically important. There are well established benchmarks in the fsQCA literature here (more technical detail can be found in the chapter appendix), and computer software aids our analysis, but put simply the goal is to find configurations of sets that are highly consistent with the high (or low) spending outcome. (e.g., whether the combination of religiosity AND traditional family values is likely to produce low family spending.) With a two-step approach identification of analytically important relations adds an additional dimension to the analysis because in the second step only combinations of factors that are analytically significant proceed to the second stage. However, in order to adapt the approach of Schneider and Wagemann (2003, 2006) for our purposes we deviate from it in a number of key regards. Perhaps the most crucial deviation is that we treat it as a process for identifying *pathways* towards outcomes in either the 'high family policy spending' set or its negation (which we dub 'low family policy spending'). This process involves, as we move from step to step, breaking our analysis into sub-samples representing different pathways based on configurations identified in the preceding step; in effect, we perform separate QCA investigations for each pathway. In addition, our injection of a third step obviously deviates from their two-step model, but we also include data from multiple time points in the final step to capture its short-term nature. We also ascertain whether short-term political and economic factors create 'exit routes' from the general paths we identify. Figure 3.1 provides an overview of our approach with a fictional example alongside it.

	PROCESS	SIMPLIFIED NOTIONAL EXAMPLE
STEP ONE Remote factors *i.e. Welfare regime influence*	Test consistency of each regime membership with high and low family spending outcomes	The **Lunar welfare regime** is analysed. Membership of this regime is found to be consistent with **low family policy spending**. The regime covers eight countries in our sample.
STEP TWO Intermediate factors *i.e. Cultural influence*	Within each regime separately test all combinations of societal values to see whether consistent with dominant outcome identified in step 1. Analytically significant combinations found within each regime proceed to step 3	Two combinations of societal values in the Lunar welfare regime are found to be consistent with low family policy spending Group A: **strong traditional family values** and **strong conservative norms** combine; three cases in Lunar regime share these features Group B: **strong religiosity** and **strong conservative norms** combine; three cases in the Lunar regime share these features
STEP THREE Proximate factors *i.e. Political and Economic influences*	For each combination of societal values within each regime identified as significant test whether all combinations of political and economic factors are consistent with high and low spending outcomes. For each regime type as a whole test whether political and economic influences provide and 'exit route' from the dominant family policy spending outcome	In Group A in Lunar regime **left government** is consistent with high family spending, pointing to a short term exit route from the long-term pattern when (a) these societal values are present over medium term and (b) a left government is in power In Group B in Lunar regime political and economic factors do not influence outcomes: spending remains low largely irrespective of levels of growth or the party in government In Lunar regime *as a whole* **left government** combined with **strong economic growth** is consistent with high family policy spending, pointing to a key exit route in the Lunar regime; under these conditions the influence of longer term influences is weakened

FIGURE 3.1 *Overview of three-step approach*

We should stress again the modest nature of our goals here; we devise a three-step analysis here to match our regression models and, specifically, to help us explore the ways in which our cases are configured in terms of institutional, cultural, political and economic contexts and how this overlaps with family policy outcomes. Ultimately, this helps us to better describe our data and flag areas for more detailed case analysis. In short, we use fsQCA as a tool to help us describe properties in our cases. In order to make the analysis more digestible we refrain from presenting our analysis in an overly technical fashion, instead placing stress on presenting the pathways visually and exploring the findings through exploration of the cases here and in Chapter 4. Ultimately QCA is first-and-foremost a 'qualitative' approach for it aims to achieve thick description of complex cases in order to learn more about them (Berg-Schlosser et al., 2009); that software packages allow for complex computations should not be reason for pursuing a 'push-button' logic at the expense of theoretical and empirical reflection (Skaaning, 2011: 405). However, in the chapter appendix we provide more technical details and formal solution formulae.

Findings

Welfare regime effects overall

In step 1 we analyse the influence of the distant factors – that is, welfare regimes – on family policy spending. Two of the ideal types stand out as having a very strong and consistent influence on the level of spending: the Social Democratic regime with a high family spending outcome and the Southern European regime a consistency with a low family spending outcome. These strengths of the links are such in these cases that we might describe the welfare regime as being a dominant influence on spending in these types. These findings are consistent with our regression model findings, which reported significant associations (and in the same directions) for these two regimes alone. They also accord with much of the theorising in the literature. Esping-Andersen's (1999) suggested that the level of defamilialisation should be greatest in the Social Democratic welfare state type and Ferrera (1996) proposed a separate Southern European model partly on the basis of the limited degree of state penetration in the provision of welfare in the region. Indeed, with regard to the latter type, the commonly presented view is that 'in Southern Europe, the state "locked" into the family unit the responsibility for the provision of care and social protection, thus, minimising the employers' and the state's political and economic costs for societal reproduction' (Papadopoulos and Roumpakis, 2013: 206).

In the remaining two regime types the picture is more complex. In the Liberal regime there is a relatively high consistency with a low family spending outcome but is much closer to the cut-offs used in fsQCA to establish consistent relationships exist, implying factors other than the regime have more influence in shaping outcomes than in the Social Democratic and Southern European regimes. That membership of the Liberal regime is closely tied to low public spending on family policy would tie with Esping-Andersen's (1999) suggestion that defamilialisation is relatively modest because of the limited role of the state in the Liberal regime, but that the consistency is close to the border of our threshold perhaps hints that there is a degree of diversity in this regime with respect to family policy provision. That the level of spending is low but less consistently low than in the Southern European regime also accords with our regression findings. Meanwhile, in the Conservative/Corporatist regime the picture is very mixed indeed and there is no consistent link to either a high or low family spending outcome, suggesting a very weak regime influence for this type. Our regression models also struggled to identify a regime effect for this type. Perhaps, though, this inconsistency is consistent with theorising on this regime type: Esping-Andersen (1999) predicted the state would play a subsidiary role in family policy, so we might expect variations in state provision based on variations in the capacity of local non-state actors to deliver provision, while Taylor-Gooby (2004b: 219) noted that this regime faced particular challenges in adapting to new social risks because 'The responses to new social risks do not sit comfortably within the established structure of the corporatist regime'. Indeed, in the sample of countries he examined (which was restricted to European states), he noted variation in the extent to which welfare states had been adapted in this regime, with France standing out as exceptional in terms of developing pre-school and childcare policies.

Analysis of the distant factors represented by welfare regimes demonstrates the continuing relevance of welfare regimes in key areas, but also leaves some questions unanswered. Taylor-Gooby's (2004b) observations on how welfare regimes are adapting to new social risks perhaps provide a useful context for the overall picture here; he concluded the Social Democratic regime has the most extensive policy frameworks, the Liberal regime is rapidly responding but with a bias to private schemes, the Southern European regime is moving slowly and remains reliant on family, while the Conservative/Corporatist regime also moves slowly with negotiated political compromises necessitated by corporatist politics. This also hints at the significance of broader non-regime level factors in shaping change beyond the regime level. Analysis of the intermediate and proximate factors for each of the four pathways (i.e., for each regime type) ought to help fill some of the gaps here. It is to this we now turn.

Social Democratic and Southern European regimes

Given the very strong regime effects identified in the Social Democratic and Southern European regimes it is useful to discuss these routes together. Indeed, for both of these regimes (Figure 3.2) the picture is, in many regards, rather straightforward once we consider intermediate and proximate factors because of the strong regime effects. Nonetheless some interesting findings are identified. In both regimes we find traditional family values have no consistent impact on policy outcomes, with strong and weak family values spread throughout cases in both regimes. In each regime we can see cases where traditional family values are strong (Norway and Sweden; Greece and Italy) and where they are weak (Denmark and Finland; Portugal and Spain); we will explore this issue in more depth below and in Chapter 4. Our other societal values are consistent in both regimes, but the two are mirror images: in the Social Democratic regime the combination of low conservative norms and low religiosity[7] is fully consistent with high family spending, while in the Southern European regime it is the same picture in reverse. Indeed, the regime effects are so strong in these regimes that other factors seem to play a supporting role – and there are no consistent exit routes into the low (for Social Democratic) or high (for Southern European) spending types.[8]

In Chapter 2, we reflected on the role that conservative social norms might play in shaping family policy but we noted then that while bivariate analysis suggested a clear negative correlation between conservative social norms and family policy spending, our regression models found no such link; across these two regimes the strength of this societal value is fully in line with expectations. Importantly, we also see religiosity

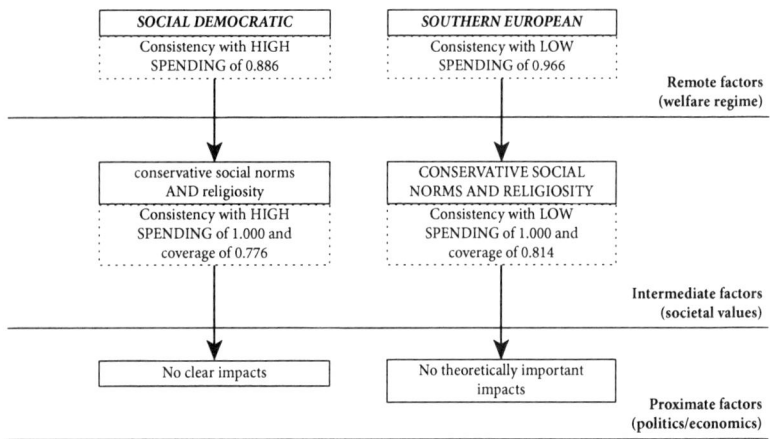

FIGURE 3.2 *Intermediate and proximate factors in the Social Democratic and Southern European regimes*

Note: UPPER CASE denotes IN set, lower case denotes OUT of set

aligned in the same way. Though we must acknowledge that there is a difference between the influence of religiosity and the influence of specific religion(s), what we observe here ties with suggestions in the literature on the role of religion in shaping welfare states (see van Kersbergen and Manow, 2009 for an overview). Davie (2012: 591), for instance, argues that 'the state–church cleavage [...] can still be felt in much of southern Europe, where the welfare system remains rudimentary', stressing the role of the Catholic Church in limiting state expansion into areas it regards as central to its own purpose, particularly the family. With respect to the Social Democratic regime, Morgan (2009: 58) argues that a historically rooted process whereby the transfer of responsibility for the family from church to state was facilitated by the fusion of the two meant that from a relatively early period 'Secularization [...] shaped the conceptualization of women with rights independent of their familial ties' and suggests that 'It is of little surprise, then, that in many Nordic countries the state would take an active role in promoting gender equality and dismantling the male-breadwinner model in the late 20th century'.

Liberal regime

Membership of the Liberal regime is consistent with membership of the low family spending type, but less strongly than for the Social Democratic or Southern European regimes meaning other factors come into play more clearly as we move to consider intermediate and proximate factors (Figure 3.3). We should note that there is no clear (medium term) route into the higher spending set based on societal values alone but it appears that proximate factors are able to become influential in facilitating a more generous level of spending. Indeed, we can see an 'exit route' from this low spending path whereby a left government increases chances of membership of the high spending set for countries within the Liberal regime.[9] In terms of real world governments, the key examples that fit this profile are what might be labelled as the 'Third Way' governments of the late 1990s/early 2000s headed by Tony Blair in the United Kingdom and Helen Clark in New Zealand. This is interesting insofar as some present these Third Way governments as an attempt to reinvent traditional Social Democratic politics under the banner of a 'social investment' model in which increased expenditure on early interventions and stronger attempts to support female participation in the labour market are emphasised over more traditional social protections (see Morel, Palier and Palme, 2012: 17–19).

However, the picture is more complex than this because societal values come into play before these proximate factors and there are hints that some societal values might work against left politics exerting an upward influence on spending. Significantly, in contrast to the Social Democratic or Southern European regimes, traditional family values appear influential, working against high family policy spending in the Liberal regime, but in two different pathways. Where traditional family values combines with high religiosity left politics does not mitigate against the low spending pathway – there are no actual cases in fact, perhaps hinting a deeper influence of these societal values on political coalitions – and the condition of the economy matters (the only instance in our study where it does) with scores in the low family spending set strengthened further when growth is lower. The key real world cases here are the United States of America and Ireland. In the second pathway, we see traditional family values combined with low conservative social norms with key real world cases fitting this pattern being Australia, New Zealand and Switzerland. This route is highly consistent with low spending, but we do see left politics providing an exit route though it is weaker than for the Liberal regime as a whole and the solution has low coverage (i.e., is rather uncommon).[10] What, then, might these patterns in the Liberal regime be pointing towards? There are perhaps three key points to draw out.

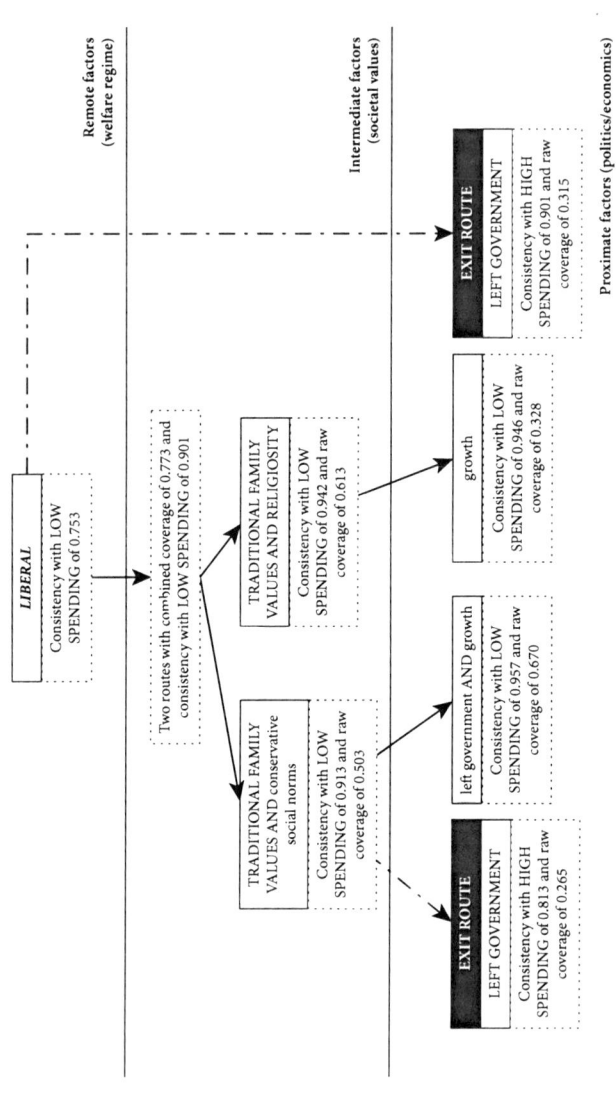

FIGURE 3.3 *Intermediate and proximate factors in the Liberal regime*

Note: UPPER CASE denotes IN set, lower case denotes OUT of set

The first key point is that our analysis seems to underline the significant role religiosity (or religion) plays in shaping distinctive policy making processes in some countries within the Liberal welfare regime type. Specifically, high religiosity seems consistent with low family policy spending. Religion is an underexplored issue in the welfare regimes literature (van Kersbergen and Manow, 2009) and much of the work to date has focused on demonstrating how religion has played a key role in facilitating the emergence of the different welfare regimes that are presumed to exist (Davie, 2012; van Kersbergen and Manow, 2009). However, a question that arises from our analysis is whether this dimension of difference might *divide* the Liberal world of welfare through important differences in societal values. For instance, in none of the Anglophone members of the Liberal regime religion is a key cleavage on which political parties have been based – in contrast to much of Western Europe where Christian Democrat parties often feature prominently – so religion might be expected to play a minor role in policy decisions. However, these same societies also show some marked differences in terms of their degree of religiosity/secularism. The United Kingdom and United States of America, for example, have widely contrasting religiosity scores in our societal values data, reflecting very distinctive social attitudes and practices with respect to the importance of God, confidence in churches and attendance at religious service. (For instance, in wave four of the EVS/WVS data only around 1 in 10 respondents in the United Kingdom say God is very important in their life, compared with almost 2 in 3 respondents in the United States.) Indeed, Quadango and Rohlinger (2009) suggest that the religious cleavage is central to much social policy debate in the United States, but operating indirectly through its impact on social attitudes and debates both within and between political parties. As they put it: 'Religious conservatives have influenced welfare state politics in the United States by defining policy debates in moral terms; penetrating deeply into the Republican Party machinery at the local, state, and national level; and forcing the Democratic Party to move in a conservative direction on social welfare issues' (Quadango and Rohlinger, 2009: 262).

The second key point is that we see traditional family values operating in a similar way to religiosity insofar they are highly consistent with low spending. Given our examples of societal values are necessarily partial and data driven measures of actual real world societal values, one reading could be that they are overlapping aspects of the same real world societal value.

However, it is interesting to note here that when our traditional family values factor it is *not* combined with religiosity there seems to be more scope (or, at least, *some* scope) for left politics to exert on upward pressure on family policy spending. Moreover, as we note in other regimes, the two are not always present together, so there are reasons to conclude the two are overlapping but distinct societal values. One conclusion may be that strong traditional family values will carry more weight in policy debates when the degree of religiosity in a country is higher because 'responsibility' for the family is a key area of contestation between church and state and so a key area in which religious institutions will seek to exert their influence. We might also add that when there is more confidence in churches – a key aspect of our religiosity factor – that the intervention of religious institutions in political debates will likely carry more legitimacy.

The final key point is that left politics may be particularly significant in the Liberal regime. As we point out above, Esping-Andersen (1999) expected the state to play a minimal role in promoting defamilialisation here and Taylor-Gooby (2004b) concluded Liberal regime countries were rapidly developing policy responses to new social risks but that the level of change was constrained by a reliance on market-based approaches. In other words, the dominant approach in this regime is expected to be one where state intervention is modest. Our fsQCA analysis confirms this, but also suggests that left wing governments have been able to deviate from this pattern on consistent basis (as have a good number of non-left governments, but they do so much less consistently). Our regression models presented identified left politics as playing a role in supporting higher levels of family policy spending, but it might be suggested that while the regression models demonstrated how left politics can shape differences in the (quantitative) degree of spending across all nations and regimes, our fsQCA points to a more conceptually significant qualitative shift in spending (from a 'low' to a 'high' spending type) that left politics can facilitate in the Liberal regime and perhaps hints that policy frameworks are more malleable to shorter term political agendas in this regime than others, for in none of the other regimes can such a consistent influence be detected.[11]

Conservative/Corporatist regime

Finally we come to the Conservative/Corporatist regime (Figure 3.4). The regime effect appears weak in this type, with cases split across high

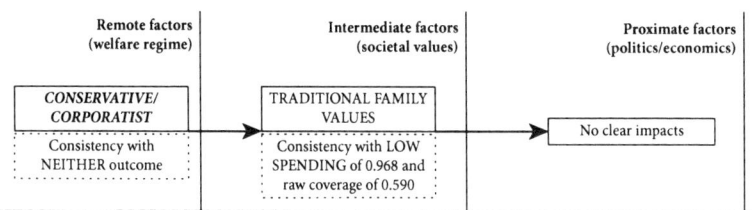

FIGURE 3.4 *Intermediate and proximate factors in the conservative/corporatist regime*

Note: UPPER CASE denotes IN set, lower case denotes OUT of set

and low spending outcomes. In fact, the fuzzy set analysis struggles to find any consistent set relationships across all of our distant, intermediate and proximate factors in this regime type, identifying just one, that strong traditional family values are highly consistent with low spending in the Conservative/Corporatist regime though we should note this solution's coverage of the low spending Conservative/Corporatist nations set is modest so other recipes leading to low spending exist that we do not find with our limited range of factors. The key real world cases falling into this pattern are Germany and Japan, though whether the latter should be deemed a member of this welfare regime or an alternative East Asian regime is a moot point (see Chapter 1 – it probably should not and the link is weaker still if Japan is excluded). It is worth underlining that many cases in this ideal type end up in the high spending set but there are no clear routes to this that can be identified at regime level; the absence of strong traditional family values, for instance, does not guarantee a higher level of spending.

Why are the results so unclear for this regime type particularly when compared to our regression analysis? One reason may be that regime effects are in fact very weak here; so weak, in fact, that we might question whether talk of a Conservative/Corporatist regime grouping is relevant to family policy. Indeed, in her recent review of work–family policies in Western Europe, Morgan (2009: 57) argues, with respect to key Conservative/Corporatist cases, that a significant historically rooted bifurcation in policy frameworks can be identified that is rooted in 'patterns of religious practice, religious divisions, and related political conflict [in the late 19th/early 20th century] that [has had] lasting significance for gendered aspects of the welfare state'. More specifically, she argues that entrenched patriarchal familialism limited state involvement in the family in continental Europe, but that anticlericalism successfully challenged this position in some countries (she cites France and Belgium as key examples, Italy as one where forces were strong, but the impact limited), whereas in others (she cites Austria, Germany and the Netherlands) Christian Democrats bolstered the traditional view and squeezed the challenge from the left. As she puts it: 'in countries such as France and Belgium, where anticlerical forces challenged the hegemony of the Catholic Church, the state expanded its responsibility for children's education and family well-being, and later proved pragmatic, rather than moralizing, on the issue of working mothers. In much the rest of continental Europe, in contrast, public policy would discourage mothers from working while their children were young, an approach that has deep historic roots and has proven slow to change' (Morgan, 2009: 84).

What Morgan's analysis implies – and this is arguably consistent with the findings we have presented so far – is while there is a sufficiently consistent and coherent set of policy frameworks around old social risks such as unemployment to group the usual set of countries together under the Conservative/Corporatist welfare regime banner, this is not the case for new social risks represented by family policy. This, in turn, reflects significant differences in the nature of welfare policy making and politics in these two policy areas and of the power of different actors involved in these spheres.[12] There are two further and more specific implications for our study. The first is that, if Morgan is correct, then it underlines an important point about the key role societal values play in shaping or modifying welfare regimes. At a minimum we can suggest that there is clear interplay between welfare regime, societal values and policy outcomes that appears to be shaping cross-national variations in family policy in key ways.[13]

The second implication of Morgan's analysis is that, if correct, it also suggests that 'hard coding' countries as members of specific welfare regime types at the start of our three-step fsQCA was wrong headed when examining family policy and that, in fact, we ought to have explored alternative possible groupings as the first step of our analysis. We have some sympathy for this view but note that our task at the outset of the book was to explore how culture might interact with commonly established welfare state types rather than to establish a new set of groupings. Nonetheless, we have recoded our data set for some post-hoc analysis with two new groupings: one representing Belgium and France as full members, with Italy at the cross-over point; the other with Austria, Germany and the Netherlands as members. The former group is consistent with high family spending as Morgan's thesis would suggest but not significantly so unless Italy is dropped from the grouping; this provides some degree of support for Morgan's thesis with regard to what we might dub the 'anticlerical' grouping within the Conservative/Corporatist regime. Analysis of intermediate and proximate factors adds nothing of substance, though we might note that both cases feature low scores for traditional family values. For the second grouping, by contrast, there is no consistent link with either high or low spending and inspection of the societal values (which are rather mixed) adds no further clues for this group. Overall, this provides some degree of support for Morgan's thesis and we return to this in Chapter 4.

Conclusion

There are undoubtedly limitations in the analysis we have undertaken in this chapter, many of which arise from our attempt to match the approach undertaken in our regression analysis as closely as possible, including the variables used to create our sets and the time periods they cover. That we developed a new application of fsQCA in order to accommodate our established analytic framework, rather than revising our analytic framework in order to accommodate an established fsQCA approach, will also raise the eyebrows of some readers. There are also the standard questions that can be asked about all QCA studies around issues such as the calibration of sets and the application of consistency tests. It has been noted that QCA generally has a weak spot with respect to *time*; breaking our analysis into three steps that separately examine long-, medium- and short-term influences was an attempt to address this, but we should acknowledge that this is not a fully satisfactory treatment of the temporal dimension, not least because the crucial issue of *sequencing* (the *order* in which events occur) is not fully addressed by our approach (Pierson, 2004). We will try to address some aspects of the temporal dimension in Chapter 4 when we explore some key changing trends.

However, detailed reflection on how our findings match existing theories, key cases and empirical trends shows that they sit well with existing evidence and this, in turn, lends plausibility to our approach. Moreover, despite some limitations arising from so doing, in matching our fsQCA with our regression model we have been able to probe questions around how societal values influence welfare policy making in ways that we would not otherwise have been able to do so. In particular, in combining a quantitative linear analysis with a closely matched three-step fsQCA we have been able to highlight some of the complex non-linear and iterative processes at the heart of the culture-welfare nexus. We end the chapter by drawing out some of these processes.

Firstly, welfare regime effects are often strong but are not always so. We see what appear to be strong regime effects in the Social Democratic and Southern European types, reasonably strong (but not immutable) regime effects in the Liberal regime but no consistent effect at all in the Conservative/Corporatist type.[14] At the same time, our findings also provide some challenges to the welfare regime argument, at least when applied in a simplistic manner. Our analysis of the Liberal regime seems to suggest that societal values play an important role in shaping important differences *within* the regime, most notably religiosity seeming to be key in dividing lower spending countries like the United States of America from higher spending ones like the United Kingdom. More broadly, the analysis of the Conservative/Corporatist regime suggests that this type may be ill-conceived (or weakly specified) with respect to family policy, failing to capture important (culturally rooted?) factors that shape cross-national policy variations.

This hints at a second point, which is that our analysis underlines that deeply embedded historical-institutional factors can shape contemporary societal values that in turn shape policy outcomes in any given area of policy. So, for instance, in the Social Democratic and Southern European regimes, the levels of religiosity and conservative social norms seem likely to be tied to longer term influences around religion, the church and established positions about the authority of the church and state in the sphere of the family. In the Corporatist/Conservative regime there are some indications the same is true, especially with respect to the cluster of countries Morgan (2009) identifies as having had a strong anticlerical response in the late-19th/early-20th centuries. In other words, we can see the enduring influence of the more abstract notions of culture that we characterised as 'macro' level in Chapter 1. However, this does not negate the value of our in-between approach to exploring culture but, instead, strengthens it insofar as the societal values that matter in each area of policy are likely to vary: while religiosity might be significant in some contexts for family policy, optimistic values may be more important for support for the unemployed and so on. Our in-between conception of culture *should* sit in-between the macro- and micro-level conceptions (see Chapter 1), not just in theoretical terms but also in acting as bridge between the two in the real world.

Thirdly, our analysis also suggests that *which* societal values are important appears to be context dependent, not just with regard to policy area but also with regard to each country's historical-institutional legacy. For instance, we find that traditional family values is consistent with low spending outcomes in two regime types, but does not have a consistent influence in two others. This perhaps reflects the different policy battles that exist in different regimes with their differing welfare systems, but also likely reflects the subtle ways in which historical-institutional legacies mobilise bias by shaping which groups have power and so which issues are more likely to rise up the policy agenda. In other words, because welfare politics differs across countries, so too do the influential societal values. At this same time, though, we should note that the interaction between policies and our societal values data might operate in the direction of policy context affecting values data. For instance, our traditional family values factor score is in large part based on responses to the question of whether marriage is an outdated institution, but the nature of marriage varies across countries on the basis of different policy frameworks, including issues around who can marry, where, on what basis and with varying rules in terms of how a marriage can be dissolved. Reponses to the question of whether marriage is outdated seem likely to be in part contingent on these policy differences and even for the same individual could vary over time as a consequence. Indeed, as Camarero (2014) demonstrates we can observe rather different values underpinning public conceptions of marriage across Europe, so much so that we can meaningfully talk of different (normative) models of marriage existing. This gives us a further reason to be cautious when interpreting data and we reflect more on both the practical and methodological implications of this issue in Chapters 4 and 5.

These arguments about how the significance of specific examples of societal values varies across context, and how welfare regime-societal value shape each other, come together in our final point. In Chapter 2 we noted a number of puzzling features in our quantitative analysis of family policy spending:

▸ Despite a priori assumptions that traditional family values ought to be influential in shaping family policy our regression analyses could not detect how and where this might be so.

- Graphical analysis and correlation analysis suggested that conservative social norms ought to be influential, but regression analysis provided only limited support for this conclusion. In addition, the direction of influence in the regression model was not as a priori assumptions would lead us to expect, showing a positive association with family policy spending rather than the negative influence expected.
- Religiosity appeared influential in our models, but we faced a puzzle regarding the negative influence on generosity of this societal value and the seemingly positive (though not significant) influence of membership of the Conservative/Corporatist regime when the two are often seen as interlinked in key theories.

We asked at the start of this chapter whether fsQCA methods might help address the puzzling findings and we believe they do, showing that:

- Traditional family values do appear consistent with low family spending in the Liberal and Conservative/Corporatist regimes, but are not consistent with any outcome in the Social Democratic and Southern European regimes.
- Conservative social norms are not consistent with high family policy spending; indeed they are consistently low in the consistently high spending Social Democratic regime and consistently high in the low spending Southern European regime.
- Religiosity is influential, but perhaps in more complex ways than the regression models can detect. In the Liberal regime it seems to play a key role in creating a firmly low spending path. It is consistently low in the consistently high spending Social Democratic regime and consistently high in the low spending Southern European regime, but does not appear influential in the Conservative/Corporatist regime. However, with respect to the latter, we find some support for theories that break this grouping into different clusters based on historic conflicts between church and state.

Chapter summary

This chapter makes three key points:

- Using fsQCA methods alongside regression based analyses can provide useful insights, particularly when the small number of

cases under investigation prevents more sophisticated regression techniques from being deployed.
- Welfare regimes and societal values interact with each other in complex ways. Contemporary societal values often reflect (at least partially) deeply rooted historical-institutional legacies. This can make disentangling the culture–welfare nexus a difficult task.
- Whether societal values are influential, and the impact they may have, seems likely to be context dependent. This is so not only across different policy areas, but also across countries within a specific policy area. Consequently, there may be times when a particular societal value may be influential in one regime type, but not in another. This creates challenges for linear forms of analysis.

We noted at the outset that our aim was to use fsQCA as a bridge between our variable centred regression analysis and some more detailed reflection on our cases. We have injected a good deal of reflection on cases in this chapter, but space has limited the depth of discussion. In our final substantive chapter we will offer a lengthier examination of some of the key cases, trends and issues highlighted in Chapters 2 and 3.

Appendix

Set calibration

- **High family policy spending:** Boundaries are established by reference to descriptive statistics capturing the long-term picture (1981–2008) but with an eye on 'natural' breaks in the data. 1% of GDP represents fully out, 3.5% fully in, 2.5% the cross-over. This places a similar number of cases fully in and fully out, with a clear break between the first cases above and below the cross-over (Belgium 2.55%, Germany 1.98%).
- **Intermediate factors:** Averages factor scores computed across all time points for each country provided the basis for these sets. (Not all cases have values for all years, adding some noise: see our FigShare site for data coverage details.) Factor scores are arithmetically derived so have no clear conceptual meaning; we therefore calibrate these set arithmetically using a direct allocation method that codes the top case for each set as 1 and bottom as 0 with values in-between allocated based on their distance between the top and bottom cases.

▸ **Proximate factors** (Party composition of government and economic growth): We use five-year averages around the four waves of the EVS/WVS, matching our regression models. Cabinet composition data (scale of 1–5) is used to capture the presence of a left government. Fully out is coded at 2.5 (indicating an average position as close to dominance of right wing parties [2] as to a balance of power between left and right [3]), fully in at 5 (left wing hegemony) and the cross-over at 3.5 (as close to dominance of left wing parties [4] as to a balance of power between left and right [3]). The economic growth set is coded to capture 'clearly growing economy' and was created by reference to long-term averages: 5% fully in, 1% fully out, 3% (around the long-term average) the cross-over.

Software usage

We used Longest and Vaisey's *fuzzy* program for Stata (Longest and Vaisey, 2008). It has many advantages (chiefly integration with Stata) but limitations around necessity tests and the ability to compute intermediate solutions when performing Boolean reductions (Thiem and Dusa, 2013: 88). Its functions in part represent Longest and Vaisey's interpretation of, and preferred approach to performing, fsQCA. There are two key implications for our study. Firstly, using it means we are also following Longest and Vaisey's preferred approach: see Longest and Thoits (2012) for a useful empirical illustration of Longest's use of fsQCA that informs our approach a good deal. Secondly, one of the features of QCA is it that allows for reduction of multiple overlapping configurations to more parsimonious solutions using the Quine-McCluskey algorithm. Though such reductions are robust arithmetically when using *fuzzy*, theoretically important combinations can be missed so manual post-estimation of solutions is sometimes necessary. The way the package operationalises this algorithm meant manual checks of output from *fuzzy* were necessary when there was good reason to believe the assumptions built into the package might have oversimplified findings. This increases the scope for human error of course.

Set relations

The most significant decisions in our fsQCA are probably those concerning how we determine which combinations of factors are deemed analytically important in influencing our outcome at each of the three steps; at step 2 this also entails determining which combinations of societal values proceed to step 3. Primarily this is done via examination of the consistency scores for each configuration: these scores represent the extent to which a configuration is sufficient for producing the outcome. Ragin (2008) suggests that it becomes somewhat difficult to maintain that a set relation exists when scores are below 0.75, but Schneider and Wagemann's two-step approach (2003, 2006) operates on the basis that scores of 0.70 or above are acceptable, partly because using two steps replaces complex combinations with simpler ones that are less likely to be consistent. They also require configurations to have at least one case present and a significance level of 0.05 or below. We employ a consistency level of at least 0.700 (and significance level 0.05 or below), with the exception being for welfare regimes that are presumed to exist as a generalised remote (and, so perhaps, inconsistent) influence on family policy. We also examine the coverage indicator, which shows the amount of an outcome explained by a specific configuration; solutions with very low coverage but high consistency were deemed to be empirically less significant and dropped from the analysis.

We deviate from the two-step approach in key regards, treating it as a process for identifying *pathways* towards membership of either the 'high family policy spending' set or its negation ('low family policy spending'). In each step we break our analysis into sub-samples representing different pathways based on configurations identified in the preceding step; in effect, we perform separate QCA investigations for each pathway. That our welfare regimes are mutually exclusive ideal types necessitates fragmenting our sample from step 2, where we perform our analysis based on separate sub-samples (one for each regime) as we look to establish which configurations of societal values influence the policy outcomes in each regime. At this juncture our approach is fairly consistent with Schneider and Waggeman's with the very crucial exception that we do not test whether welfare regimes consistently influence outcomes. (We are instead guided by a priori assumptions that regimes are important.) Injection of a third step clearly deviates from their model. In Step 3 we analyse the impact of proximate factors based on further sub-samples for each *configuration* of societal values found to be important *within* each regime type; we also examine the influence of proximate factors within each regime as a whole in order to ascertain if generalised 'exit routes' from the dominant spending path exist. We boost what would be small samples in the third step by including data from four time points for each case; this also allows us to detect shorter term influences on outcomes and better match our regression models.

Summary of solution pathways

i To HIGH FAMILY SPENDING outcome:
SOCIAL DEMOCRATIC•conservative norms•religiosity → HIGH FAMILY SPENDING
LIBERAL•FAMILY VALUES• conservative norms•LEFT → HIGH FAMILY SPENDING
LIBERAL•LEFT → HIGH FAMILY SPENDING

ii To LOW FAMILY SPENDING outcome:
SOUTHERN EUROPEAN•CONSERVATIVE NORMS •RELIGIOSITY → LOW FAMILY SPENDING
LIBERAL•FAMILY VALUES•RELIGIOSTY → LOW FAMILY SPENDING
LIBERAL•FAMILY VALUES•RELIGIOSTY•growth → LOW FAMILY SPENDING
LIBERAL•FAMILY VALUES• conservative norms•growth•left → LOW FAMILY SPENDING
CONSERVATIVE/CORPORATIST•FAMILY VALUES → LOW FAMILY SPENDING

Notes

1. There are a number of variants of the approach – crisp set QCA (csSA), multi-value QCA (mvQCA) and fuzzy set QCA (fsQCA) – but the latter is our focal point here (see Ragin, 2008; Rihoux, 2011 for overviews).
2. The number of logically possible combinations is 2^k, where k is the number of sets under consideration. Each combination may correspond to several real world cases, which in turn allows an insight into the causal relationship between specific configurations of conditions (i.e., sets) and any given outcome. Indeed, QCA tests each possible configuration of conditions together to uncover whether these are sufficient or necessary for the outcome (Ragin, 2008).
3. Taking these two principles together we have *multiple conjunctural causation*.
4. Given that one of our aims here is to use fsQCA techniques to fill in some of the gaps unfilled by our regression-based analysis we place some limiting

constraints on our approach here. The key limitation is that the sample of countries analysed, the time points, data sources and the variables included in the analysis are largely pre-determined by the processes outlined in Chapters 1 and 2. However, we believe that utilising a mixed-methods research design enhances the robustness of our overall approach and aids both analysis and theorising. We will, though, reflect on some of the limitations arising from this approach when discussing our findings.

5   This approach addresses the challenge of limited diversity because the highest possible number of logical remainders (z_{max}) that can exist is radically reduced: with a one step fsQCA $z_{max}=2^k - 1$ (where k is the number of sets), but in a two step fsQCA $z_{max} = 2^{k_1} - 1 + 2^{k_2} - 1$, so with 8 factors in the first approach z_{max} would be 255 but if the 8 factors are broken into two steps with four in each then z_{max} is a mere 30 (Schneider and Wagemann, 2006: 762).

6   One advantage of this is that it allows us to capture changes in the outcome set that occur over time – there have been considerable shifts in the level of family policy spending in some cases – and then to see how far proximate factors have allowed cases to deviate from their longer term oaths.

7   Technically non-membership of the high conservative social norms and high religiosity sets but we simplify the narrative here.

8   Some combinations of proximate factors pass the set tests, but are of either such low coverage or inconsistent meaning to add anything significant to the picture.

9   There is a consistency of 0.901 and coverage 0.315 for this combination; simplifying a good deal, this is a little like saying around 9 in 10 left wing governments in the Liberal regime have high family policy spending, but that only around 3 in 10 Liberal regime governments with high spending are left wing, what we might call a sufficient but not necessary condition for high family spending in the Liberal regime. We should note that a good number of non-left governments have also delivered high spending too in this regime but do so less consistently.

10 We might note that, in this regime, the absence of left government combined with low economic growth is highly consistent with low family spending and has a much higher coverage as a solution.

11 There may be a temporal dimension here insofar as many of the examples of left-governments come from the late-1990s/early 2000s when the social investment model gained purchase across much of the OECD and so this effect may disappear in the future.

12 Morgan (2009) views the differences between the groups she identifies to be sufficiently fundamental to label them *gendered welfare regimes*.

13 We might even go so far as to say it implies societal values can be so deeply embedded in the historical-institutional context of a nation that attempts to develop independent measures of societal values and historical-institutional context will be challenging.

14 That we see consistent combinations of our key societal values in the two types where regime effects are strongest could raise questions about the direction of welfare regime-culture influence, though that clear regime effects for these types have been found in other policy areas where other societal values are influential gives us reason to believe these are genuine welfare regime influences.

4
Exploring the Culture–Welfare Nexus: Key Trends, Key Cases

Abstract: *In this chapter we focus in greater depth on some key trends and key cases highlighted in chapters. More specifically, we examine four issues: the Conservative/Corporatist regime puzzle; the Liberal regime bifurcation; the meaning of traditional family values; and, the significance of optimistic values. In exploring these issues we demonstrate how more detailed exploration of case study evidence may help understand how the culture–welfare nexus operates in practice, offering a more nuanced perspective than is possible through broad-brushed macro-level comparisons alone. We also explore some of the methodological challenges uncovered in Chapters 2 and 3, pointing to refinements to our approach that may be taken forward in future research.*

Keywords: culture; welfare state models

Hudson, John, Nam Kyoung Jo and Antonia Keung. *Culture and the Politics of Welfare: Exploring Societal Values and Social Choices.* Basingstoke: Palgrave Macmillan, 2015. DOI: 10.1057/9781137457493.0009.

Introduction

In the final substantive chapter, we dig deeper into the data that our analysis of the culture–welfare nexus is based on. However, rather than offering what would be a very lengthy exploration of each case or indicator, our focus here is very much driven by the findings of Chapters 2 and 3, examining in more depth some key trends and cases (or groups of cases) that our earlier analyses suggested may be of particular interest. Consequently, this chapter has a somewhat 'episodic' feel, but deliberately so, for our aim is to look more deeply at a small number of issues. More specifically, we examine four issues: the Conservative/Corporatist regime puzzle; the Liberal regime bifurcation; the meaning of traditional family values; and, the significance of optimistic values. In doing so we not only tease out some of the finer points of culture–welfare nexus, we also point to some possible priorities for future research and highlight some areas where methodological refinements might improve our approach in future work.

The Conservative/Corporatist regime puzzle

In exploring family policy we found something of a puzzle with respect to the Conservative/Corporatist regime insofar as no clear regime effects were detectable. Morgan's (2009) claim that two distinct family policy frameworks have developed in continental Europe as the consequence of historic church–state power struggles was advanced as a possible explanation. Interestingly, a cluster analysis of all societal values data for the Conservative/Corporatist cases alone produces a grouping that appears to fit with Morgan's thesis (see Table 4.1): we see France and Belgium clustered together as she suggests; they are joined by Luxembourg, which she did not explore, but in terms of state–church power conflicts we might usefully note that Messner (1999; cited in Minkenberg, 2003) groups it alone with Belgium in terms of its church–state relations. Meanwhile, each of the countries that she suggested appear on the other side of this bifurcation are also grouped together – Austria, Netherlands and Germany.[1] This provides some further support for the suggestion that there are distinctive differences *within* this regime type that need to be further understood; quite what it means for our own study is a tricky question to disentangle. On the one hand it could be read as evidence of

TABLE 4.1 Cluster analysis of societal values data for Conservative/Corporatist regime

Cluster	Members
1	Belgium (90; 99; 08) France (90; 99; 08) Luxembourg (99; 08)
2	Austria (90; 99; 08) Germany (90; 99; 08) Netherlands (90; 99; 08)

Dendrogram using ward linkage
Rescaled distance cluster combine

Note: Ward's method with standardisation. All examples of societal values included: conservative social norms; inter-personal tolerance; optimistic values; permissive values on adherence to laws; political activeness; political orientedness; religiosity; and traditional family values.

a fundamental flaw in the notion of a Conservative/Corporatist welfare regime that spans this grouping of countries. On the other, if societal values are viewed as operating independently from welfare regimes (as is our contention), then it may hint at ways in which sub-groupings of countries can emerge *within* regime types that have relatively coherently clustered societal values that in part reflect important and deeply rooted institutional differences within regimes (and in turn shape policy differences).

However, we ought to be cautious here, for our cluster analysis is based as it is on all of our examples of societal values; selecting fewer provides a more dynamic picture.[2] If we only select the societal values included in our regression and fsQCA analyses of family policy – conservative social norms, traditional family values and religiosity – we see much less stability in the groupings over time (Table 4.2). In fact, if we assume that these three societal values can be read as representing a more general notion *social conservatism*, then the pattern we see is one of the Conservative/Corporatist countries becoming progressively *less* conservative over time. In Table 4.2, we include a 'conservatism index' computed by simply averaging the factor scores for these three societal values; a higher score indicates a higher degree of conservatism. As can be seen, the clusters become *more conservative* as we move from Cluster 1 down to 4; what is less obvious at first glance is that all the countries move from *more to less conservative clusters* over time, but this is captured more clearly in the data visualisation in the bottom right panel of Table 4.2. As this shows, the Netherlands is a long-established member of the *least conservative* grouping, arguably unsurprisingly so given its place in Esping-Andersen's (1990) framework is ambiguous (Hudson, 2012), some classifying it as Social Democratic rather than Corporatist/Conservative (e.g., Goodin et al., 1999). Indeed, comparative analysts have debated how to classify the country for some time, it sitting uneasily in many typologies because it features elements that are both corporatist and social democratic (Cox, 1993; Therborn, 1989). We can also see that France has long been on the less conservative side of this grouping, consistent with Morgan's (2009) argument about the different values that have existed here with respect to the roles of church and state in the sphere of the family.

In Table 4.2 we can also see an incremental drift away from conservatism in Germany.[3] This might be seen as particularly significant given that Germany was identified as the key example of the Conservative/Corporatist regime in Esping-Andersen's (1990) study. A number

TABLE 4.2 Cluster analysis of societal values data for Conservative/Corporatist regime – conservative social norms; religiosity; traditional family values

Cluster 1	Cluster 2	Cluster 3	Cluster 4
France (99; 08)	Austria (08)	Belgium (90)	Austria (90; 99)
Netherlands (all years)	Belgium (99; 08)	Germany (90; 99)	Belgium (81)
	France (81; 90)	Netherlands (81)	Germany (81)
	Germany (08)		
	Luxembourg (99; 08)		
Mean conservatism index score: −0.55	Mean conservatism index score: −0.40	Mean conservatism index score: −0.14	Mean conservatism index score: 0.01

Visualisations of Clusters

Note: Ward's method with standardisation.

of analysts have suggested that Germany's welfare regime has been fundamentally reformed since the turn of the century as social policy has adapted to new social risks and a post-industrial economy, Bleses and Seeleib-Kaiser (2004) even talking of a 'dual transformation' of the German welfare state as protection for 'old' social risks has weakened while protection for 'new' social risks has strengthened. In an analysis of childcare politics, Naumann (2012: 164) highlights the role specific societal values have typically played, pointing to secularization and an associated weakening of religious cleavages in voting as 'factors conducive to the development of postindustrial childcare policy'. But, in the case of Germany, she also points to unique factors, chiefly reunification; debates around family policy that laid bare some differences in societal values in the East and West of the country, for at the moment of reunification 'most East Germans held gender norms that differed considerably from the West German conservative family image and were more in line with the adult-worker model' (Naumann, 2012: 173). Indeed, she suggests that a ground-breaking expansion of childcare approved shortly after reunification was passed with much grumbling from within the conservative government's own ranks. This, in turn, hints at another key issue she highlights in Germany's case, which is that the shifting landscape of societal values has altered both voting behaviour and the electoral strategies of the key political parties. Indeed, she places great stress on the shifting and intersecting political cleavages, with religion, class and gender all playing an important role. As we noted in Chapter 2, Manow and Emmenegger (2012) suggest that similar processes are at play across much of the Conservative/Corporatist regime.

Bleses and Seeleib-Kaiser (2004: 152) argue that recent changes to its welfare state mean 'that Germany can no longer be accurately described or characterised as a conservative welfare state'. Interestingly, while the general trend across all the countries we examine is one of declining social conservatism, the rate of decline is sharper in some regime types than others (Figure 4.1): while there has been a rapid shift downwards in our 'conservatism index' scores for the Liberal and Conservative/Corporatist regimes, the changes have been more modest elsewhere (we have added an East Asian grouping comprising Japan and South Korea to capture the slow change in these countries). The impact of this is that the index scores for the Conservative/Corporatist regime are, in the late 1990s and 2000s, well below the average for our sample as a whole and much closer to those of the Social Democratic regime than they are

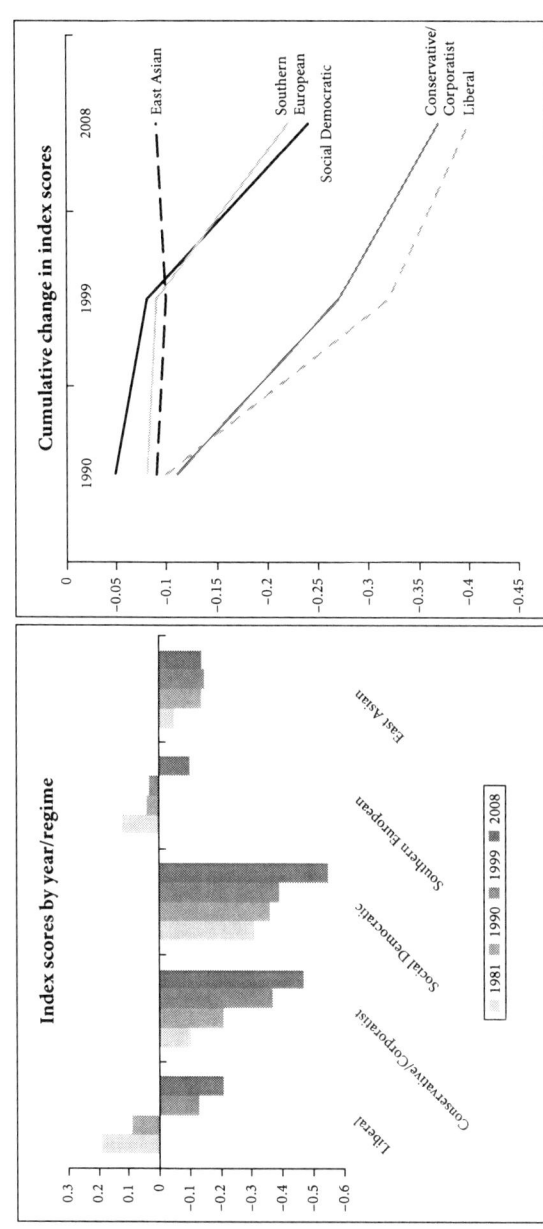

FIGURE 4.1 *Conservatism index scores by regime*

to those of any other regime type, a contrast to the 1980s/early 1990s when the scores for the Conservative/Corporatist regime were very close to average and further from the Social Democratic regime score than those for the (relatively socially conservative) Southern European and East Asian types. In short, the shift in these values seems notable in this regime and raises the question not only of whether Germany ought still to be labelled as 'conservative' but in fact the type as whole; this is perhaps particularly so given the normative value-based stance the term 'conservative' implies.

This slow dissolving of socially conservative values in the Conservative/Corporatist regime may go some way towards explaining why our regression and fsQCA models struggled to disentangle the societal values – welfare regime interactions for type, particularly for family policy where the most relevant societal values appear to be in a greater state of flux and the established policy frameworks requiring more fundamental reform than is the case for other regimes. Indeed, Häusermann (2012: 122) hints at this, suggesting 'The saliency of family policy reform is particularly high in continental Europe, where all countries – except France – have been relying on the 'old' male breadwinner model family policy [...] way into the 1990s'. As we noted, in Chapter 2, Taylor-Gooby's (2004a) exploration of how welfare states were adapting to new social risks concluded that the 'modernisation' challenges faced by this regime type have more profound implications for policy than is the case for other regimes but the politics of reform in a corporatist system means that the pace of change is typically rather slow. Interestingly, Palier (2012) has suggested recent reforms mean that we can no longer observe the 'frozen landscape' of fixed policy frameworks Esping-Andersen (1990, 1996b, 1999) once identified in this regime. This does not necessarily mean that we have recently seen sudden and dramatic shifts in policy; indeed, Palier (2012: 236) stresses that 'though the changes only became fully apparent over the past decade, they must be understood as the culmination of a longer reform trajectory'. In their analysis of Germany, Bleses and Seeleib-Kaiser (2004) similarly stress the evolution over frameworks over time. All this would tie in well with the suggestion that gradual shifts in societal values have helped facilitate a gradual shift away from traditional policy frameworks.

However, we should avoid jumping to simple and deterministic conclusions here. Societal values seem likely to have fed into reform processes, but will not only interact with other factors in so doing, but do so in ways that might defy simple analysis, even if only because the finer details of policy settlements are so often loaded with complex multiple meanings that they do not easily map onto one set of values as opposed to another. This is even so when considering broad questions such as whether a 'dual transformation' of the German welfare state has taken place as flagged by greater emphasis on family policy as opposed to traditional social protection for the unemployed. As Häusermann (2012: 113–115) suggests, presenting the picture as one of old versus new social policy may be too simplistic, for a more nuanced analysis might find old and new social policy responses *within* each area of policy. She suggests, for example, that in family policy we find examples of old social policies (e.g., cash benefits aimed at social protection) *and* new social policies (e.g., child care that aims to be a social investment). This, in turn, means that we might see complex value positions supporting not just a shift towards more family policy but towards specific *types* of family policy. We might also expect political actors to try to exploit these different potential readings of policy change in order to build new political coalitions that seek to adapt to changing societal values without compromising too heavily. Interestingly, Naumann (2012: 175) notes that growing support for the dual earner model in the 2000s created political challenges for the Christian Democrats in Germany; ultimately they embraced the dual earner model, but crucially they did so through a 'strategic reframing of childcare as an economic, rather than a gender equality issue', permitting a reconciliation of their 'old' and 'new' values.

The Liberal regime bifurcation

Our fsQCA exploration of family policy flagged a seemingly important bifurcation in the Liberal regime. The key dividing point seemed to be around religiosity, but if we perform a cluster analysis on the 'conservatism index' explored above then we can observe a broader bifurcation across the type more generally (Table 4.3) with Canada, Ireland and the United States on one side and Australia, New Zealand, Switzerland and the United Kingdom on the other.[4] Even accounting for a general reduction in social conservatism over time does not alter this picture; we can usefully observe that the mean conservatism index for the first group is *higher* in 2008 (i.e., more conservative) than for the second group in 1981. This underlines the arguments presented in Chapter 3 about the role differing patterns of societal values may play in shaping *within regime* differences.

TABLE 4.3 *Cluster analysis of societal values data for Liberal regime: conservative social norms; religiosity; traditional family values*

	Broad grouping		Sub-groupings		
Cluster	Members	Mean conservatism index	Cluster	Members	Mean conservatism index
1	Canada Ireland USA	0.16	1a	Ireland (81, 90) USA (81)	0.49
			1b	Canada (90, 99, 08) Ireland (08)	−0.03
			1c	Canada (81) Ireland (99) USA (90, 99, 08)	0.11
2	Australia New Zealand Switzerland UK	−0.27	2a	Australia (99, 08) New Zealand (99, 08) UK (81, 90)	−0.22
			2b	Switzerland (99, 08) UK (99, 08)	−0.36

DOI: 10.1057/9781137457493.0009

Visualisations of clusters

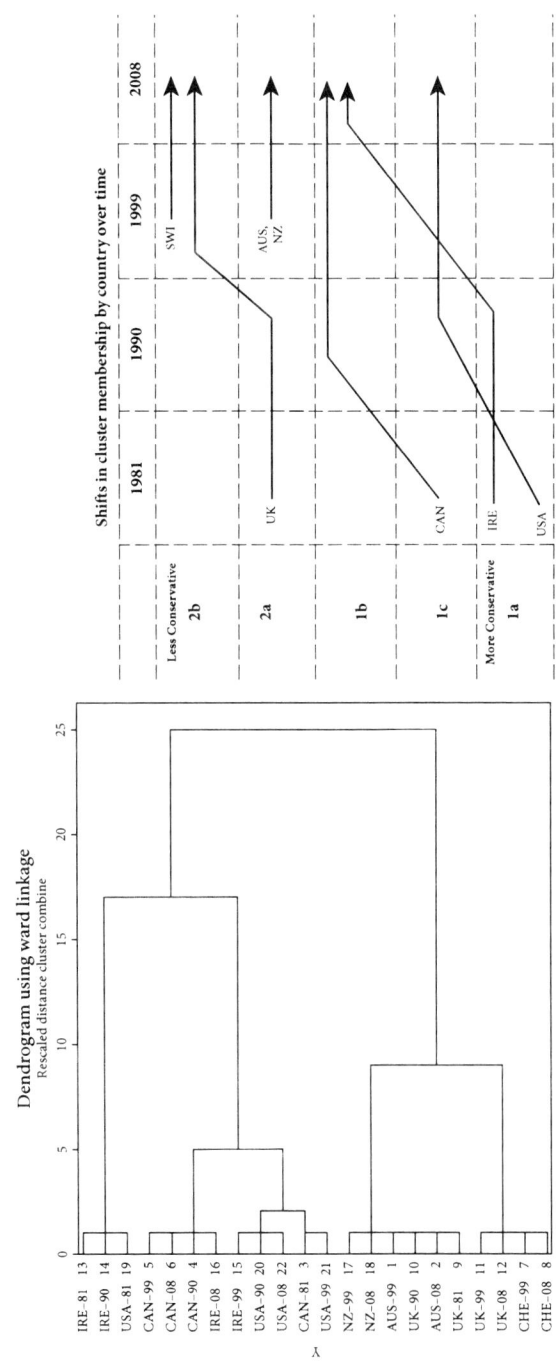

Note: Ward's method with standardisation.

One of the limitations of our fsQCA exploration was the treatment of time, with societal values analysed on the basis of medium-term average scores. Because societal values are theorised as being broadly stable over the medium term (Chapter 1) – and our examples of them extracted from the EVS/WVS data on this basis – this decision ought not to impact heavily on our findings, but it does risk missing cases that deviate from the norm in having more rapidly changing societal values. As Table 4.3 shows there are some cases that fit this pattern with regards to the 'conservatism index' in the Liberal regime. A more fine-grained reading of the cluster analysis might suggest five groupings rather than two: we label them 1a–1c (which we might view as three sub-groupings of the Canada/Ireland/USA cluster) and 2a–2b (which we might view as two sub-groupings of the Australia/New Zealand/Switzerland/UK cluster). In so doing we gain some insights into how societal values have shifted over time; in the bottom right panel of Table 4.3 we present a graphic that highlights movement in cluster membership from more to less conservative groupings over time, showing that most countries have moved into less conservative clusters over time. However, while an upward shift is commonplace, the case of Ireland stands out in moving across three clusters, capturing what appears to be a particularly deep shift in societal values in this case. Interestingly, Ireland is also the standout case in this regime in terms of changing family policy spending (Figure 4.2), moving from below regime average spending in 1981 to well above regime average spending in 2009 (and this despite a rapidly rising regime average).

We might usefully contrast Ireland with the United States here for two reasons. First, in terms of spending, the United States began the 1980s with a low level of family policy spending, but unlike Ireland has not seen its expenditure shift upwards in the period since; indeed, it has remained consistently low (Figure 4.2). Secondly, our fsQCA model suggested that, when examining the picture over the medium term, a combination of high religiosity and high traditional family values worked strongly against high family policy spending in the Liberal regime. This was the picture for both Ireland and the United States over the medium term, but we noted in Chapter 3 that in examining medium-term averages that we risked missing some cases where significant short-term shifts had occurred and Ireland is such a case. Crucially, however, this is so not just with regards to Ireland's level of spending but also these two examples of societal values, its scores for religiosity and traditional family values

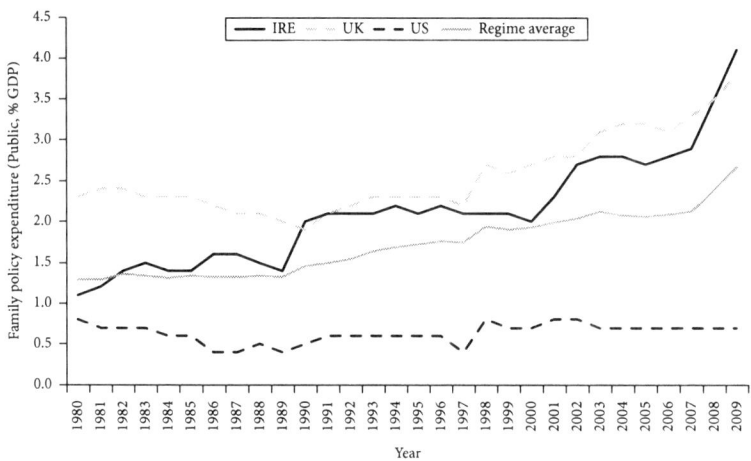

FIGURE 4.2 *Ireland's rapidly rising family policy expenditure*

declining sharply in the 1990s/2000s, particularly so for traditional family values. It might be argued therefore that Ireland provides a clear instance of where a relatively rapid change in societal values has facilitated a rapid change in policy. Indeed, in a review of family policy in Ireland, Fahey and Nixon (2014: 134) note that normative conflict between liberal and Catholic views of the family has been a feature of family policy debates in the country, concluding that the 'resolutions arrived at on these issues by the 1990s were quite liberal relative to what had prevailed up to the 1960s'.

It is tempting to take this as a confirmation of the pivotal role that societal values play in reshaping social policy. However, Fahey and Nixon (2014: 134) also hint at the underlying complexity of policy change and, indeed, values shift in actuality, arguing that while a more liberal set of values influenced family policy in Ireland by the 1990s, 'on some issues (especially abortion but also, to a lesser extent, divorce), [views on the family] were still at the conservative end of the European range'. We noted in Chapter 2 that an examination of spending alone can be misleading both because it tells us little about where spending is allocated and because some key policies do not require large expenditures. A more fine-grained analysis of Ireland's changing family policy shows that while some areas (such as cash benefits) have rapidly expanded, others (such as child care) have not (see OECD, 2011). Moreover, one of the most significant debates in this sphere of policy has surrounded abortion; though changes have occurred since the early 1980s, Ireland's strict laws around abortion continue to mark out the country as unusual in European terms, reflecting the ongoing influence of Catholic values. Importantly, in this particular instance, current policy frameworks also demonstrate the added complications for analysis arising from the influence of institutional structures, for having seen the risk to traditional policy frameworks presented by changing social norms, a socially conservative coalition of actors successfully campaigned for insertion of a 'protection of the right to life' amendment into the constitution in the 1980 (Fahey and Nixon, 2014). Given such amendments require approval by a referendum, this has added a complex layer of veto points to policy-making in this area, not only in requiring further referenda to permit fundamental policy change, but also bringing the Supreme Court into play in this area of policy (Fahey and Nixon, 2014). This underlines that while in some areas of policy a rapid change in societal values can feed relatively directly into changing policy frameworks, in others governments face bigger institutional barriers in changing policy and so we might reasonably expect a less direct connection between changing societal values and policy outcomes.

We can add a further layer of complexity here too by observing that the connection between broad societal values and public opinion on specific policy issues (which we characterised as the 'micro-level' conception of culture in Chapter 1) may be mediated by specific national contexts. In the case of abortion policy in Ireland, we should note that there have been further referenda and constitutional amendments since the 1980s but the outcome of these referenda have reflected an underlying social conservatism – compared to European norms – in this particular area of policy that is somewhat out-of-line with the declining social conservatism captured in our societal values data for Ireland. This likely reflects the heightened significance of normative issues in this area of policy for some of Ireland's key political actors. On a similar note, the fuzzy way in which changing societal values may permeate the details of family policy is also evident in the area of cash benefits where, according to Fahey and Nixon (2014: 132–3), the growth in family policy spending was until very recently either unconnected to a pro-female employment agenda or even reinforced traditional parenting patterns (see OECD, 2011 also). Again a focus on spending alone cannot pick up these important nuances in the detail of policy.

This reinforces the point made in the previous section about the complexity of selecting appropriate outcome measures in comparative analyses of 'new' social policy: a simple focus on spending or programme rules cannot tell us everything and, ultimately, the thick description of case studies is key in confirming the validity of broad brush hypotheses concerning the culture–welfare nexus. It also underlines some of complexities we face in interpreting the meaning of societal values, not least because seemingly common cross-national patterns of societal values may have subtly different implications in different countries because of their unique policy contexts. However, these important provisos aside, our underlying contention that changing societal values can help us understand why Ireland and the United States have taken divergent family policy paths since the early 1980s seems a reasonable one. This is particularly so when we consider that, like in Ireland, family policy in the United States has been a zone of normative conflict, particularly abortion law which has been entwined with Supreme Court rulings and is a touchstone issue for some political groups. Indeed, in the United States it has even permeated debates around health care reform with conservatives repeatedly blocking plans to extend the coverage of publicly funded health care provision whenever proposals might have the potential to permit state-funded access to abortion on a pro-choice basis (Quadango and Rohlinger, 2009). In short, while governments in both countries have faced a complex set of institutional constraints in the family policy sphere, in Ireland shifting societal values have meant that religiosity, and associated debates around traditional family values, have not been so central in driving political competition in the way they have in the United States (see Chapter 3; Quadango and Rohlinger, 2009). In other words, the 'softening' of these key societal values seems to have been important in facilitating a political climate more conducive to expanding state provision in the sphere of family policy.

Traditional family values

The above discussion is connected with the third topic we explore in this chapter: the meaning of traditional family values. We noted a number of puzzles with regard to this societal value in Chapters 2 and 3, particularly that it seemed to perform less strongly as an explanatory factor for family policy difference than might be expected. Figure 4.3

displays trends for this societal value for our core sample of countries, each chart also displaying the average for this value for the 16 OECD countries we have full data for. The average score for our traditional family values factor has dropped over time, suggesting that these values have weakened over time. Bar occasional outlier cases in each type, across most of the welfare regimes the story is one of traditional family values either remaining static or more usually declining over time. The key exception to this story, which runs contrary to expectations, is the Social Democratic regime where we actually see a good degree of relative *strengthening* of traditional family values over time. As Figure 4.3 shows: in Demark traditional family values strengthen as the country moves from well below average to around average; in Finland we can see the same pattern; in Norway scores are around average in 1981 and 2008 – so lower at the end point than the start point of our data set – but they move to well above average in the 1990s; and, Sweden is very similar to Norway, starting around average and ending at just above average but with a clear above average spike in the middle of our data set. Given the consistently low levels of social conservatism in this regime, this picture seems surprising to say the least. What, then, might be behind this?

On the basis of an analysis of EVS data for all EU states, Camarero (2014) demonstrates that we can observe rather different values underpinning public conceptions of marriage across Europe, with normatively different models of marriage existing. For instance, there is clear variation between EU countries on questions such as whether faithfulness is important to marriage, whether affairs can be justified, whether divorce is acceptable and whether a long-term stable relationship is necessary to be happy (Camarero, 2014). She develops a series of ideal types of marriage through analysis of such data, but her typology offers few immediate clues to the Scandinavia puzzle; Norway is excluded from her analysis by virtue of not being an EU member, but this proviso aside her findings demonstrate clearly that Scandinavia is home to the least traditional view of marriage in the European Union, both in terms of the highest proportion of people viewing marriage as a 'contingent' (i.e., flexible, negotiated) institution (Sweden, Finland and Denmark occupy the top three positions in the European Union here), but also in terms of the model of marriage with the lowest proportions supporting the traditional institutional model (Camarero, 2014: 455). Not only does her study underline the socially liberal view on marriage found in the Social Democratic regime, we cannot ascertain any significant

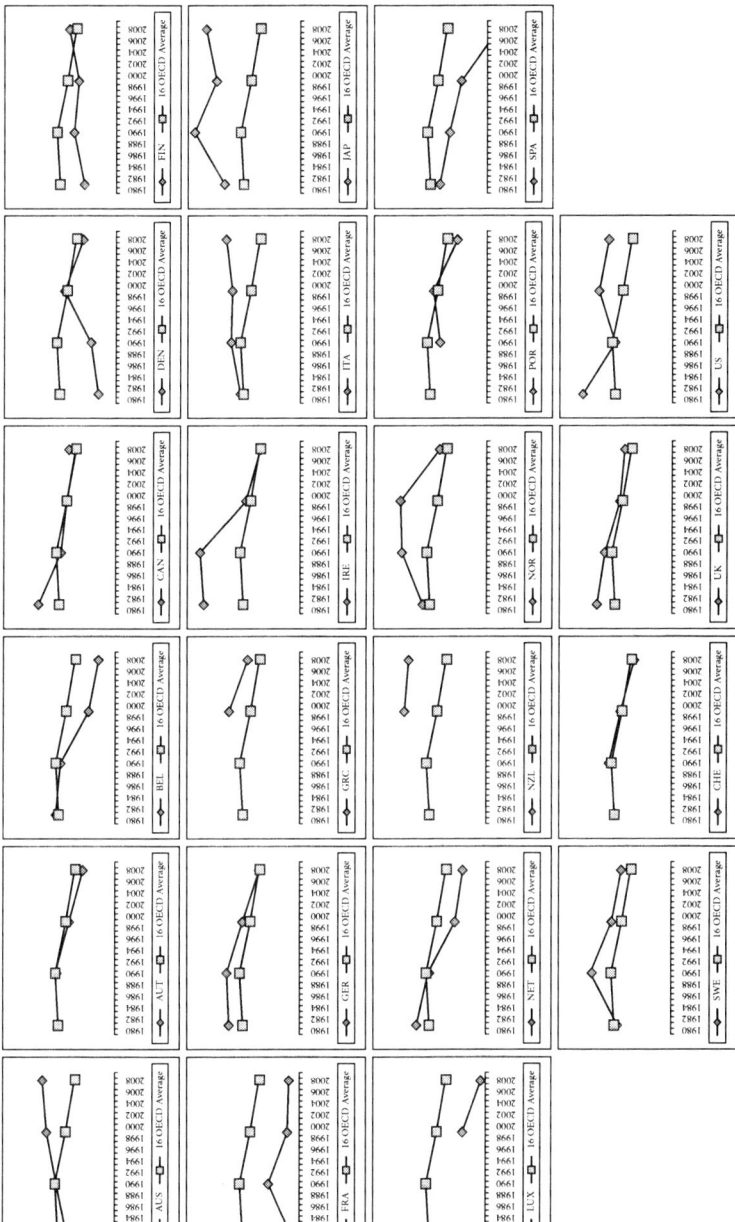

FIGURE 4.3 Traditional family values scores by country, over time

differences between Scandinavian countries in Camarero's study either, with the three cases she examines ranked closely together in almost all dimensions.

What her study does suggest, however, is that responses to one of the two EVS/WVS questions that feed into our traditional family values factor scores – is marriage an out-dated institution? – seem likely to be contingent on the social and legal norms around marriage in a country. Across the Social Democratic countries the proportion disagreeing that marriage is an out-dated institution is around or above the average for our sample of countries at each time point of the EVS/WVS. Indeed, the proportion is well above average in many instances, particularly since the 1990s, with around 4 in 5 people disagreeing with the view that marriage is an out-dated institution across the four countries in 2008. We need to ask, however, whether this carries the same meaning as the near 4 in 5 people holding the same view in Greece or Italy, where Camarero's (2014: 455) study suggests the most traditional institutional view of marriage is held by 39% of people compared to just 8% in Sweden or 12% and 13% in Finland and Denmark respectively. Throw into the mix that in 2008 neither Greece nor Italy had laws permitting same-sex registered partnerships or marriage, while the Scandinavian countries were the first in the world to introduce same-sex registered partnerships (beginning with Denmark in 1989, the others following in the 1990s/early 2000s), and the complicated multiple meanings that can lurk beneath responses to this question are evident. Indeed, it arguably tells us much that both sets of countries have high support for the view that marriage is not out-dated yet have such different laws on same-sex partnerships/marriages.

This offers a useful reminder of how the meaning of our societal values scores may be context dependent rather than universal. It also helps us understand why some of the Social Democratic nations may *appear* more conservative than they are on the basis of responses to this question. It perhaps suggests too that the framing of the question around whether marriage is 'out-dated' is problematic given the possibility of social and legal 'modernisation' exists; indeed, Ohlsson-Wijk (2011) observes that there has been a revival in marriage rates in Sweden in the 2000s, confounding both what appeared to be the long-term trend in the country that led the world in the decline in marriage rates from the 1960s onwards *and* broader theoretical predictions around the features of social modernisation. Changing values are a big part of this story in Sweden;

as she puts it: 'The meaning of marriage and partner relationships seems to have changed [...] and marriage is no longer the conventional form of union formation that it was when the transition in values and behaviour started' (Ohlsson-Wijk, 2011: 194). We will return to the methodological implications of this in the next chapter.

Interesting though these issues around marriage may be, they do not help us to understand why Norway and Sweden ended in our strong traditional families fsQCA set, or Denmark and Finland out of it, for there is little to distinguish between the four in terms of their responses to the question of whether marriage is out-dated; indeed, Sweden tends to show slightly lower proportions disagreeing with the 'marriage is outdated' view (see Figure 4.4). Instead, and perhaps surprisingly so once again, the explanation for this – and for the relative hardening of traditional family values in the Social Democratic regime – is to be found in attitudes towards lone mothers. In the cases of Sweden and Norway both have years where the EVS/WVS data show their disapproval for lone mothers well above the average for our sample as a whole and it is this that pushes them into our high traditional family values set over the medium term.

Once again it may be that the meaning of responses to this question will vary according to the cultural and policy context in which a survey respondent is located. It is worth clarifying at the outset the precise wording of the question, for it outlines a rather specific scenario of lone parenthood: 'If a woman wants to have a child as a single parent, but she doesn't want to have a stable relationship with a man, do you approve or disapprove?' There is, evidently, a normative tone to this question, but from our perspective as analysts exploring the implications of societal values for welfare states, it does not tightly match normative debates around lone parents and putative dependency on welfare that have featured in some countries, so we should not read across scores for this question directly in this way. Moreover, the policy context is important here, for Norway and Sweden have child benefit packages that strongly compensate lone parents in order to reduce their risk of poverty (Bradshaw and Finch, 2002: 11; Skevik, 2006); in fact, their systems are easily among the most generous in the OECD in this regard and the continued cross-party support for these arrangements makes it difficult to read the data as representing a deep societal desire for introducing punitive welfare arrangements for lone parents. Indeed, Skevik (2006: 244) argues that while the Scandinavian nations have relatively high

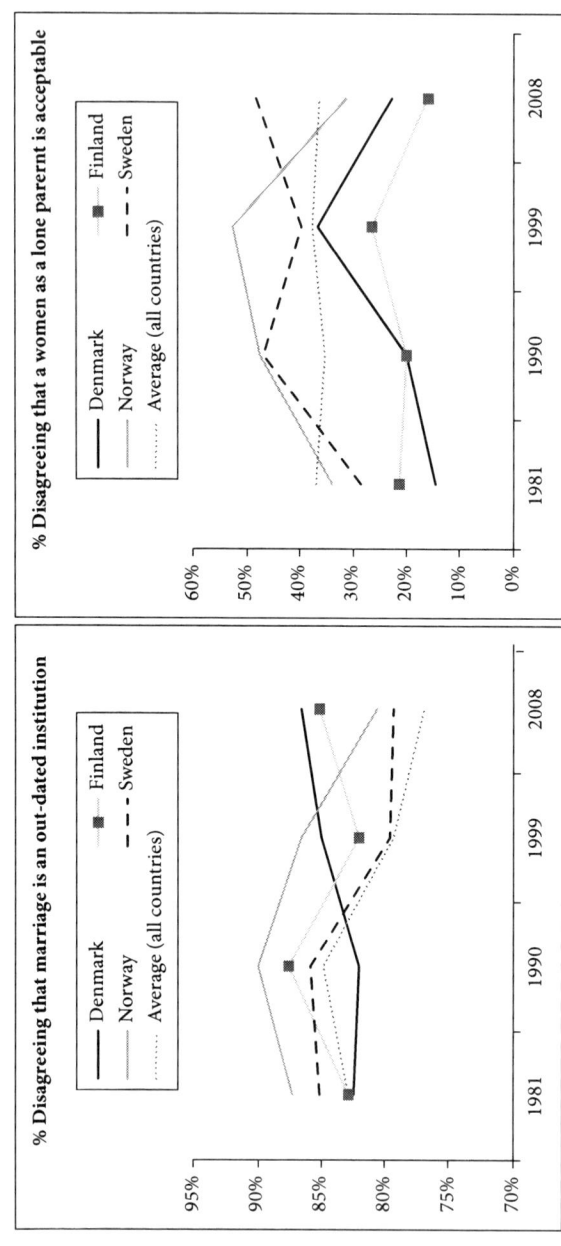

FIGURE 4.4 Raw EVS/WVS responses for components in traditional family values factor, Social Democratic countries versus whole sample average

proportions of lone parent households 'there has at no point been a moral panic regarding this fact'.

Nonetheless, the figures are striking and it would be wrong to dismiss them out-of-hand. While Skevik is clear that there has been no moral panic over the issue, she also notes that key reforms have taken place in both countries. In Norway, where the EVS/WVS data for the 1990s show well above-average scores for disapproval, the package of support for lone parents was by far the most extensive across the OECD at this time (Bradshaw and Finch, 2002; Skevik, 2006: 247). This comparative generosity was displayed not just in benefit payment levels, but also conditions of receipt, with separate benefit arrangements for lone parents that were not tied to labour market activation programmes (Skevik, 2006). A separate benefit structure for lone parents meant that there were some controversies around when benefits should be withdrawn when new relationships formed, with centre-right parties expressing concerns about marriage penalties existing. By the late-1990s, Skevik (2006: 253) says, 'The time had come for a thorough review of the benefit arrangements for lone parents'. Major reforms were introduced in 1998 and 1999, with labour market activation becoming a key focus (e.g., those with children over three years old would be required to seek at least part-time work or education), time limits were placed on some benefits and rules around co-habitation tightened (Skevik, 2006). Whether this had an impact on the pattern of EVS/WVS data for Norway is hard to say, but we can observe that the proportion disapproving of lone parenthood declines sharply between the 1999 and 2008 surveys, going from well above average for our sample of countries to below average. The picture in Sweden is slightly different, with above-average disapproval ratings in 1991 and 2008 separated by a dip to around average in 1999. With respect to 2008, closer inspection of the EVS data shows that there is some noise in the data for Sweden in 2008, for the survey was administered slightly differently in Sweden on this question at this time, with an 'it depends' response normally offered removed. It is impossible to know how the data would appear without this change, but when compared to earlier surveys it appears that this change provided a greater boost to the numbers agreeing, rather than disagreeing, with the acceptability of lone parenthood, so perhaps we might conclude that 1990 is the real outlying year for Sweden. If that is so, it perhaps ties with a moment of debate over policy supports for lone parents, with preferential tax treatments for lone parents coming under the spotlight before being temporarily discontinued in 1992 (with some compensating supports) and abolished altogether in 1993 (Skevik, 2006: 249). Although we would not want to place too great a stress on the links between this data and the policy changes we flag – more directly relevant data on state support for lone parents would be preferable – it does nonetheless suggest that something has happened in these two countries with respect to support for lone parents both in policy and value terms. Echoing our discussion of marriage, perhaps this too hints that societal values display policy feedback effects, with normative judgements on what is acceptable shaped in part by relevant policy frameworks. This naturally creates challenges in interpreting data: an increase in the disapproval for lone parenthood in a country with generous state support may merely be flagging that more people feel the balance of support for those cohabiting or married versus lone parents needs some minor readjustment rather than an overt stigmatisation of lone parenthood, whereas in a residualised welfare system that penalises lone parents this may not be so.

We noted at the outset of this section that the Southern European regime also displays a bifurcation in our fsQCA exploration of traditional family values. Here, perhaps, the puzzle is easier to explain. While all four countries in this regime were low spenders, Greece and Italy had strong traditional family values while Portugal and Spain had weak traditional family values. In contrast to the Scandinavian nations, Camarero's (2014) study echoes these differences: whereas Greece and Italy are among the nations with the highest proportion in the European Union endorsing the most traditional institutional form of marriage (39% in both, compared with 8% in Sweden), Portugal and Spain have comparatively low levels (29% and 20% respectively, with the EU-24 average at 28%). Laws on same-sex marriage and civil partnerships map onto our data well too: whereas (by 2008, the last year of the EVS/WVS data) Spain had already introduced same-sex marriage rights (in 2005, the first country do so) and Portugal's laws had de facto recognition of same-sex unions from 2001 (with marriage laws introduced in 2010), Greece and Italy had no laws in place for either civil partnerships or marriage. In other words, the different conceptions of family and marriage appear to have fed into different legal frameworks in these two sets of countries, but these differences would not impact in a substantial way on the spending data we examined in Chapters 2 and 3. This again reinforces the ongoing relevance of the 'dependent variable problem' in comparative social policy research (Kühner, 2007b).

Optimistic values

In Chapter 2, we found that optimistic values were positively and significantly associated with spending on unemployment, whether we looked at the share of GDP or the share of total social spending, echoing findings from our previous work (Jo, 2011). This societal value comprises responses to questions about: how much freedom of choice and control there is in life; feelings of happiness; and, satisfaction with life. Some may feel there is perhaps some degree of conceptual discordance within this factor, the freedom/control dimension differing perhaps from the satisfaction/happiness dimension; however, Flavin, Pacek, and Radcliff, (2014, *pace* Rothstein, 1998) see a clear connection between the two: 'Simply put, one is more in control of one's life if one has more security, such that to the extent that the welfare state does provide such security, it contributes to agency, which contributes to greater satisfaction with life.'

What all dimensions certainly do share, however, is they might be seen as either inputs to, or outcomes of, policy frameworks. Indeed, more normally the latter is the focus in policy studies. So, for instance, a growing body of work has explored the links between policy and subjective well-being (Pacek and Radcliff, 2008), but the presumption is generally that the direction of causality is one whereby social policies *impact on* levels of subjective-well-being. So, for example, Sjöberg (2010) uses data from the European Social Survey to conduct a multi-level model analysis of the links between unemployment generosity and happiness, finding a strongly positive link between the two. Crucially, this applies not just when examining those with recent experience of unemployment or in vulnerable jobs, but across the whole population, leading him to conclude that 'from a cross-national perspective, the generosity of unemployment benefits seems to be as important for the subjective well-being of the employed as it is for the well-being of unemployed individuals' (Sjöberg, 2010: 1297), which he surmises is likely tied to the way strong unemployment protection reduces risk and uncertainty for all members of society. Similar arguments have been made at the welfare state level as a whole. Flavin, Pacek and Radcliff, (2011; 2014) use WVS data to construct multi-level models exploring the links between life satisfaction and state size; whether examining data for 2008 (Flavin, Pacek and Radcliff, 2011) or from 1981 to 2008 (Flavin, Pacek and Radcliff, 2014), they find a positive link between the size of the (welfare) state and the level of life satisfaction. Similar to Sjöberg, these findings hold true irrespective of the income of individuals (Flavin, Pacek and Radcliff, 2011: 263), suggesting that policies protecting individuals from economic insecurity seem to have the greatest impact on happiness (Flavin, Pacek, and Radcliff, 2014). Ono and Lee (2013), in examining micro-level cross-national data from the International Social Survey Program to explore the determinants of happiness, offer a slightly different take, suggesting that social democratic welfare states 'redistribute' happiness, rather than expanding it per se, social policy boosting the happiness of some groups at the expense of others. We should note that some studies have produced still more equivocal findings (e.g., Veenhoven, 2000), but the general picture from this research is much as Pacek and Radcliff (2008: 189) conclude: 'that the welfare state, as a manifestation of government has a tangible impact on life-satisfaction and happiness'. While this body of work makes a good case for a link between optimistic values and higher welfare spending existing, it poses problems for our study insofar as the presumed direction of causality is policy impacting on societal values. There are good reasons why this should be so, particularly given the promotion of happiness and well-being has become a point for policy and political debates in recent years (see OECD, 2013b). Does this suggest that optimistic values should not be seen as representing an aspect of culture however? If it is merely an output of policy-making rather than an input, then perhaps so. Are there reasons for believing that optimistic values may act as an input into policy making?

Our method for extracting examples of societal values from EVS/WVS data (see Chapter 1) specifically isolates (dynamically) stable patterns of responses to EVS/WVS questions. In other words, there is a good degree of stability across countries and across time with regards to the patterns of survey response to the questions this factor comprises. Figure 4.5 shows the scores for optimistic values for each of our countries (compared to the average for the 15 OECD countries we have full data for); the average picture is one of gentle upward drift in the scores for the factor and the national scores have remained broadly stable once a general uplift is accounted for, more so than is the case for almost all other societal values. A general stability of data within and across nations has been noted by those specialising in the analysis

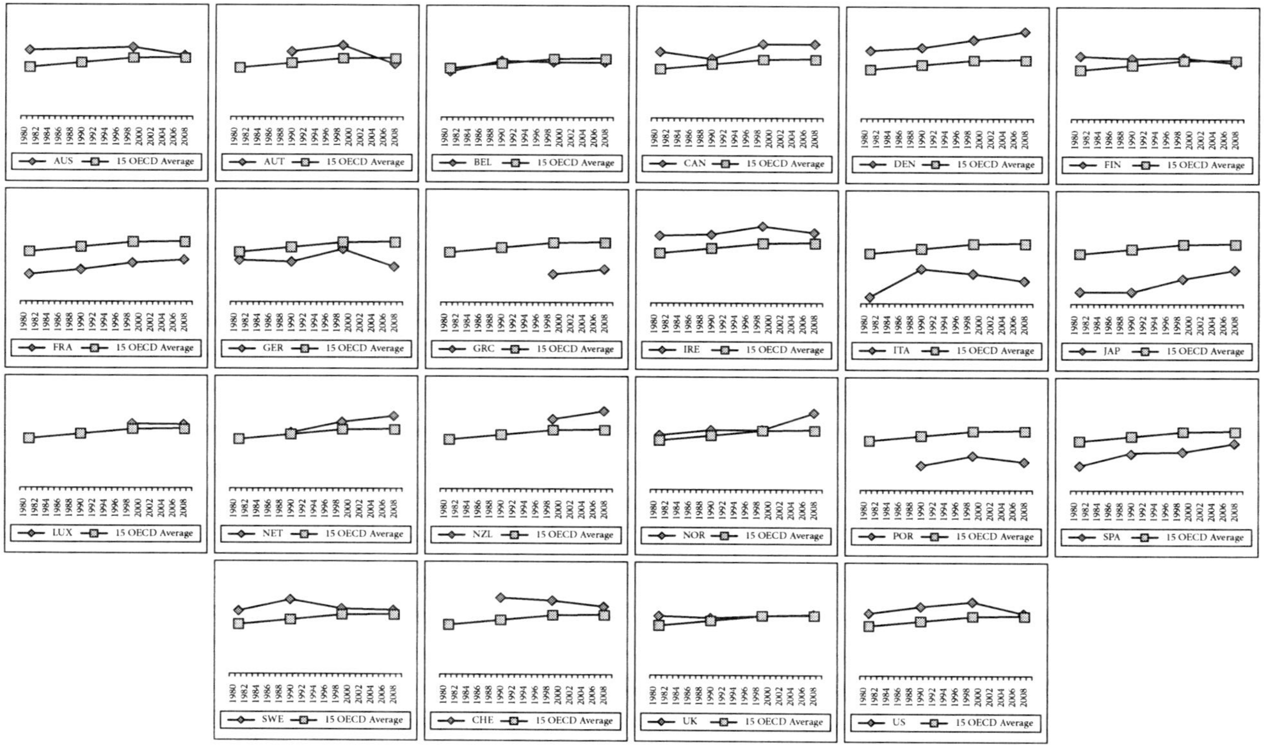

FIGURE 4.5   Optimistic values scores by country, over time

of subjective well-being data generally (e.g., Veenhoven, 2012: 348) and, indeed, that cross-national differences seem rather stable has been raised an issue when subjective well-being data is used to evaluate the impact of policy change because subjective well-being scores do not seem very sensitive to short-term policy changes (Jarden, 2011: 187). This stability in cross-national patterns of happiness has prompted much debate over whether culture influences levels of self-reported happiness and there is a well-established literature in this area (see OECD, 2013b; Veenhoven, 1987, 2012). Ordinarily, however, the culture–happiness link only feeds into debates about whether measurement errors exist in subjective well-being data, some arguing data biases arise when cultural differences lead people in different countries to respond differently to questions about their happiness in ways that do not reflect *actual differences* in levels of happiness (see Veenhoven, 2012). As Lane (2000: 31) notes:

> National differences in average happiness always interest people – who are nevertheless usually ready to dismiss them on the grounds that responses are merely reflecting cultural norms and do not reveal whether people in one culture actually feel happier or unhappier than other peoples. [...] In a colloquial phrase, is America happiness happy, that is, does the United States rank high among nations because of the high value placed upon being happy?

Lane, in common with most specialists in the area, suggests arguments about American 'happiness' are rooted more in stereotype than reality (for the United States is outranked by other nations) and that the measurement bias is not significant. Veenhoven (2012: 350) takes a strong line here, arguing cross-national differences in self-reported happiness 'cannot be denounced as mere measurement bias, nor can they be explained as a result of cultural difference in the evaluation of life [... they] denote that not all societies meet universal human needs equally well'. In making his claim he points, for example, to the fact that an analysis of the happiness of migrants shows their patterns and levels of happiness more closely mirror those of the country they have migrated to than the one they migrated from.

These commonly held positions on the happiness–culture debate not only undermine arguments that differences in optimistic values may be culturally rooted they also conceptualise well-being as *influenced by*, rather than *influencing*, policy. Some dissenting voices in the debate offer food for thought however. Interestingly, Mathews (2012) suggests that those downplaying the measurement bias issue do so, on the basis of a flawed conceptualisation of culture. Echoing some of the arguments we review in Chapter 1, but drawing on contributions from anthropology, he points out that 'Culture today, in the anthropological world, can be used in its adjectival form, but not as a noun; one can speak of something being cultural, in terms of it being socially constructed, but not of "Indonesian culture," or "the culture of Turkey"' (Mathews, 2012: 304).

This is significant because many of the attempts to empirically disprove that culture biases measurements of subjective well-being assume the cultural influence is *national* in character rather than something more nuanced: to take the language we use in Chapter 1 it is a macro- rather than meso-level understanding of culture and rather deterministic to boot. Mathews (2012) see a complex interplay of cultural, social and institutional contexts, along with individual characteristics, shaping happiness, permitting useful study of the interplay between culture and happiness, albeit his view being that statistical research needs to be accompanied by anthropologically rooted work in order to gain a fuller understanding of these processes. Approached from this direction, though Matthews does not put it like this, it is reasonable to see optimistic values (comprising aspects akin to happiness) as a malleable but sticky societal value often shaped by nationally rooted institutions.

It seems reasonable to presume that this malleability includes the potential for social policies to shape optimistic values, allowing for some reconciliation of these competing arguments. In other words, we should expect to see policy feedback in this area. Indeed, we might expect particularly complex feedback loops to exist between social policy and optimistic values. In Chapter 2, we highlighted Berlant's (2011) argument that expansion of state activity in key areas of social and economic policy 'motored' much of post-war optimism in Europe and America, but that the 'retraction, during the last three decades, of the social democratic promise' of this era (p. 12) has contributed to an 'attrition of a fantasy, a collectively invested form of life, the good life' (p. 26). At first sight this might seem like another argument that the welfare state shapes optimistic values, but her argument is more subtle, about how shared visions of the 'good life' can be sustained in the face of growing structural inequality. One aspect of her argument of particular relevance here is her analysis of what she dubs 'the neoliberal feedback loop' (Berlant, 2011: 192), whereby the growing precarity of life arising from 'neoliberal practices', including shrinkage of the welfare state and reduced job stability, 'permeates the affective environment' and so makes the social democratic post-war vision of 'the good life' seem a more distant reality than in the past. How far this picture fits with the empirical reality is a moot point – we do not have systematic cross-national data that stretches back this far to assess the claim – but her suggestion that policy feedback loops impact the *affective environment* might chime with our data given, in the round, that countries with broadly more generous welfare systems over the medium term (and those most similar to the post-war Social Democratic model) also tend to be those with the stronger optimistic values. This consideration of the way the affective environment might foster collective visions of what is politically possible perhaps echoes Pierson's (2004: 39) suggestion that path dependency may be evident not just in terms of policy structures but also in terms of patterns of belief which may be self-reinforcing to a degree too, not least because national policy frameworks and societal values are often mutually reinforcing. Intriguingly, some recent research on subjective well-being and voting behaviour (based on analysis of the United Kingdom alone) finds that those with higher levels of subjective well-being are more likely to vote for the incumbent political party (Liberini, Redoana and Proto, 2013); if these patterns repeat cross-nationally then strong optimistic values at the societal level may even help foster path dependency in policy frameworks through the ballot box.

In short, while the dominant perspective in social science research is that the dimensions comprising our optimistic values factor are *influenced by*, rather than *influencing*, social policy, there are theoretically plausible suggestions in the literature that give us reason to believe there are complex feedback loops between optimistic values and policy frameworks. Establishing proof that these loops exist is a vexed task, exacerbated by the limited timeframe for which data is available. Uncovering how such loops operate is likely, as Mathews (2012) suggests, to require in depth multi-method, multi-disciplinary research and so we cannot provide a definitive picture here. However, the stable patterns of values that exist in this sphere give us reason to believe that our optimistic values factor is something more than a mere outcome of policy and points the way to a fruitful line of exploration for future research.

Chapter summary

This chapter makes two key points:

▸ Analysis of case evidence can help us to understand key instances where our regression and fsQCA explorations struggled to explain expected culture–welfare linkages in the 'new' social policy. This includes puzzles around the role of conservative social norms in the Conservative/Corporatist regime and a complex bifurcation in the Liberal regime. In each case, changing societal values seem important in helping us understand policy change.

▸ Deeper examination of specific societal values points to some challenges that we face in interpreting quantitative cross-national information about societal values because of policy feedback effects. Not only might changing policy frameworks alter the underlying normative meaning of some societal values, but policies and societal values might influence each other in an iterative manner that produces a complex multi-directional model of causality.

These findings add strength to the 'culture matters' thesis but also point to some important future research agendas and to potential refinements to our 'in-between' approach to the analysis of the culture–welfare nexus. We turn to these issues in our final chapter.

Notes

1. Morgan also included Italy as in-between the two; we do not include Italy in Figure 4.1 because we allocate it to the Southern European regime, but adding it to the cluster analysis places it in a separate cluster altogether, further support for Morgan's thesis perhaps.
2. We should also note that there is insufficient data on some values to allow for a comprehensive analysis that stretches back to 1981.
3. We see this too in Austria towards the end of the 2000s.
4. Performing a cluster analysis on *all* our examples of societal values for this regime does not produce a similar bifurcation (with cases somewhat randomly spread amongst a large number of clusters), suggesting that the point of difference is connected to the extent of social conservatism across the regime type.

5
Conclusion: Bringing Culture 'Back In' to Comparative Social Policy Analysis

Abstract: *In this chapter we draw the book to a close, pulling together the key arguments advanced across each chapter. We suggest that there is considerable value in bringing culture 'back in' to debates about cross-national variations in social policy and that the exploration of societal values may help us to understand more not only about how and why welfare states differ but also how and why their long-term paths may change over time too. However, there are considerable methodological challenges faced in exploring the culture–welfare nexus empirically and we reflect on some of the key challenges here.*

Keywords: culture; welfare state models

Hudson, John, Nam Kyoung Jo and Antonia Keung. *Culture and the Politics of Welfare: Exploring Societal Values and Social Choices*. Basingstoke: Palgrave Macmillan, 2015. DOI: 10.1057/9781137457493.0010.

Summary of key arguments

In Chapter 1 we noted that culture is often said to be an important factor in explaining cross-national variations in welfare and has featured as an important explanatory factor in core contributions to the welfare types debate, but the role it plays in shaping cross-national variations in varying policy structures has rarely been subjected to a detailed empirical analysis. We argued that, in part, this results from complexities in conceptualising culture and developing robust 'measures' that can act as a proxy for culture in empirical analysis. We suggested that our 'in-between' approach that uses examples of societal values as a proxy for culture can address both these issues. Using our approach we extracted eight examples of societal values from EVS/WVS data. We showed that our examples of societal values do not merely capture the commonly identified welfare state types by another route, being only loosely related to common welfare-type memberships. This gave us good reason to presume that culture and welfare regimes are related but act independently of each other, providing a strong rationale for including societal values in cross-national analyses of welfare.

In Chapter 2 we used our examples of societal values as a proxy for culture in regression models. The models provided strong evidence for the 'culture matters' thesis when examining old social risks represented by unemployment spending, highlighting in particular that optimistic values are positively associated with higher levels of overall spending on the unemployed and the converse for conservative social norms. Our models provided less strong support for the culture matters thesis when we were exploring new social risks represented by family policy spending. There was fairly strong evidence to suggest higher levels of religiosity are linked to less extensive family policy provision. However, historical-institutional and political factors appeared more clearly influential in this area of policy, with membership of the Social Democratic regime and a left-wing government providing the most favourable environment(s) for expansive family policy. This led us to conclude that our models struggled to capture some of the complex interactions between culture and welfare regimes, particularly for family policy, though they pointed to many ways in which culture might be influential. We argued that supplementing our regression models with fsQCA methods may help us to dig deeper into the culture–welfare links.

In Chapter 3 we used fsQCA methods to explore culture–welfare links in the areas of family policy. The findings from this analysis showed that welfare regimes and societal values interact with each other in complex ways and that contemporary societal values often reflect (at least partially) deeply rooted historical-institutional legacies. This can make disentangling the culture–welfare nexus a difficult task. Our analysis suggested that whether societal values are influential, and the impact they may have, seems likely to be context-dependent. Consequently, there may be times when a particular societal value may be influential in one regime type, but not in another. For example, we found traditional family values to be important in restricting the level of spending in the Liberal and Conservative/Corporatist regimes, but not in the Social Democratic and Southern European regimes. The combination of values sometimes mattered too: in the Liberal regime the strong traditional family values seemed to work more strongly still against high family policy spending when combined with a high degree of religiosity. This creates challenges for linear forms of analysis because the impact of a societal value may vary according to context. We suggested that fsQCA methods may help address this and that using them alongside regression models can provide useful insights, particularly when the small number of cases under investigation prevents more sophisticated regression techniques from being deployed.

In Chapter 4 more detailed analysis of case evidence helped us to understand key instances where our regression and fsQCA explorations struggled to explain expected culture–welfare linkages in the 'new' social policy. This included puzzles around the role of conservative social norms in the Conservative/Corporatist regime and a complex bifurcation in the Liberal regime. In each case, changing societal values seemed important in helping us understand policy change. Deeper examination of specific societal values pointed to some challenges we face in interpreting quantitative cross-national information about societal values because of policy feedback effects, particularly in the area of optimistic values but also, in some countries, traditional family values. A particular issue we highlighted was that changing social policy frameworks can alter the underlying normative meaning of some societal values; this points to some of the ways in which policies and societal values might influence each other in an iterative manner that produces a complex multi-directional model of causality.

Taken together, the evidence and arguments presented across the book as a whole add strength to the 'culture matters' thesis and show that our quantitatively rooted 'in-between analysis' can help us to better understand the culture–welfare nexus. However, we have aimed to be deliberately modest in our interpretation of the evidence, aware of some limitations we face in this task, including the 'fuzzy' nature of our data and the challenges of capturing complex interactions between political, economic, social, historical-institutional and cultural contexts. Indeed, throughout the text we have highlighted areas where further research or alternative approaches might prove fruitful in unpicking the culture–welfare nexus still further. We conclude by taking stock of what we have found here and reflecting on how our findings might usefully inform future research agendas.

Capturing societal values

One of the core contributions of our text is confirmation of the utility of our in-between approach to the analysis of culture. Having replicated our earlier work (Jo, 2011) with an additional wave of EVS/WVS data we are now in a better position to judge the validity and stability of the examples of societal values we extract using this data. In this regard, it is significant that we found a strong degree of overlap between the factors extracted when using three waves of data in our earlier work and four waves in this study, for it gives us good reason to conclude not only that these factors are dynamically stable patterns of values (as required by our theorisation of culture) but that they have a reasonable degree of external validity. That said, we have acknowledged from the outset that a limitation of our approach is that it is data-driven. This is necessarily so given our rationale for developing the in-between approach, but in Chapter 4 in particular we noted some conceptual weaknesses that can flow from the data-driven approach, such as traditional family values scores being rooted in survey questions about marriage that might be sensitive to context-specific changes in policy.

However, a fifth wave of EVS/WVA data will be available soon; if repetition of the exercise again identifies similar factors then we might usefully consider whether there are sufficient grounds for relaxing our data-driven approach in order to strengthen the conceptual basis of our examples of societal values. One way this might proceed is that if a factor loosely pointing towards 'traditional family values' (for example) is again identified then we might base analysis first on the original factor scores, but then accompany this with an analysis in which a bespoke traditional family values index is developed using handpicked questions from the EVS/WVS data that best match the policy area we are exploring. In such an approach, our original method would still point us in the direction of the appropriate stable societal values, but we would also use our conceptual and case knowledge to supplement this data-driven approach. This would echo some aspects of the fuzzy set approach to constructing sets in which an interplay between data, case knowledge and conceptual knowledge is key.

Fusing multi-method, multi-disciplinary, multi-level perspectives

Modifying our approach to the measurement of societal values in the way suggested above would also allow us to modify societal values that may be particularly sensitive to complex feedback loops when this is deemed problematic. We noted in Chapters 2–4 that these feedback loops present a particular challenge to analysis of the culture–welfare nexus, especially when some of the factors we identified – optimistic values being the key example – are more ordinarily seen as *outcomes of*, rather than *inputs to*, the policy-making process. Modifying societal values in order to remove factors that are most likely to be deemed contentious in terms of the direction of causality would be one way around this.

At the same time, however, we would suggest that it is the exploration of the complex interplay between culture–policy–politics–society that provides the most fruitful future research agendas. Here we agree with Mathews (2012) that quantitative analysis can only provide us with part of the answer, not least because feedback loops between policy and societal values mean that the latter can never be seen as truly independent variables. Add in the complexity of cross-national analysis in which even factors such as language may subtly bias survey responses and the limits of relying on quantitative data alone soon become apparent. Some of the challenges here will be resolved over time: measurements are undoubtedly becoming more sophisticated and the collection of ever greater amounts of statistical information not only means that we will have a greater range of indicators to choose from in the future, but the increased the number of cases that can be included in quantitative models will permit usage of more complex regression techniques. Nonetheless, we believe multi-disciplinary, multi-method work will always add value in this area of analysis. We hope that we have shown here the value of combining macro-quantitative work with fsQCA and some limited case-based analysis. Deeper case-based analysis and subsequent refinement of regression and fsQCA models would take our understanding still further. Mathews (2012) suggests that anthropologically rooted analysis of discourses in each country under investigation can further understanding and we agree with suggestion too, though obviously this adds much complexity to the research task when many countries with many different languages are the object of investigation. In this study we have usefully drawn on research from a wide range of disciplines and sub-disciplines including social policy, politics, sociology, economics, cultural studies, anthropology, demography, religious studies. As social policy specialists, our limited understanding of some of these subject areas has no doubt limited the depth of our analysis, which would undoubtedly be strengthened by working with specialists from each area.

In addition to the value of a multi-method, multi-disciplinary approach we might add the value of undertaking multi-level analysis in the future. Our analysis has been very much on the macro-level of societal values and national policy frameworks. This is par for the course in comparative social policy analysis, particularly when welfare regimes are a focus for analysis, but it brings limitations (Hudson, 2012). Chief among these are that we might miss very important ways in which social divisions might shape values within a country, but the assumption that societal values are coterminous with the borders of nation–states is problematic in some countries where culturally distinct geographic regions may exist. It is difficult to address some of these limitations when using EVS/WVS data because of the modest sample sizes involved, but it is worth noting that a good deal of work has used multi-level regression models to explore the interplay between cross-national and national factors; in Chapter 4, for instance we pointed to interesting studies examining whether national unemployment protections interact with individual factors such as income levels, precarity of employment and recent experience of unemployment in explaining levels of happiness across nations (Sjöberg, 2010). Adding perspectives from this kind of analysis to macro-level quantitative analyses of the sort we present here seems likely to be useful.

Bringing culture back in

Sensitivity to these kinds of issues means that we have been tentative in advancing some of our detailed findings here; but the big picture 'culture matters' thesis finds strong support nonetheless. Indeed, the suggestions we advance above point to ways in which we might be bolder in exploring the finer details in future studies. The case for bringing culture 'back in' to comparative analysis of welfare seems strong, not only because we are able to shine a light on some key ways in which culture matters in this book, but also because it seems that societal values may become more significant in shaping change as some of the uncertainties of the old class politics melt as the post-industrial economy unfolds. That the frozen landscape of some welfare regimes may be melting too adds further reason to explore how societal values might shape reform processes. The suggestions we make above will help strengthen the analysis of how culture shapes cross-national differences in social policy. But still bolder research agendas exist that we can take forward as we gain more sophisticated and more extensive measures of both societal values and policy frameworks. We end by pointing to three agendas that seem likely to be particularly fruitful.

Our focus here has been on how societal values feed into policy-making, which van Oorschot (2007: 134–135) dubs the analysis of culture's *ex* ante influence: how it feeds into policy-making decisions before policies are implemented. However, he also highlights that the '*ex post legitimacy control effect*' culture can play *after* policies are implemented. Our societal values data holds potential for exploration of these effects too. So, for instance, we might usefully explore whether take up of parental leave schemes is mediated by the strength of 'traditional family values' or 'conservative social norms'. We do not undertake such an analysis here because robust cross-national data on policy take-up is thin on the ground. However, advances in data collection (e.g., the very detailed EU-Statistics on Income and Living Conditions data collected by Eurostat) and sophisticated tax-benefit micro-simulation tools that include fine-grained detail on policy provisions (e.g., EUROMOD) offers us greater potential than in the past for developing such analyses.[1]

Whether societal values impact on the take-up or acceptance of implemented policies links to a second potentially very interesting research agenda: how societal values data might be used to assist understanding of cross-national policy transfer processes. It is commonly observed in the policy transfer literature that cultural differences can be a barrier to the movement of policy lessons from one country to another; for instance, the Evans and Davies model of policy transfer (Evans, 2004, 2009; Evans and Davies, 1999) cites cross-national cultural differences as a cognitive barrier in the search for policy lessons and public opinion/attitudes as a barrier to the acceptance of ideas from abroad. Rose (2005: 93), however, is critical of the nebulous conceptualisation of culture often used in this context, arguing that such positions tend to 'imply that trying to draw lessons across national boundaries will fail. The success of a programme in a given country is ascribed to its distinctive values and beliefs or style of policy, implying that any attempt to export it elsewhere would be doomed to failure because each national culture is deemed unique. [...] However, such general statements do not identify the specific features of a culture that are obstacles to lesson-drawing.' The role societal values data might play here is self-evident. Although we acknowledge that considerable methodological and conceptual challenges exist, explorations of how and when similarities or differences in societal values have influenced the success or failure of policy transfer processes might help us to improve both theorisations of how policy transfer operates and more applied cross-national lesson drawing tools.

It is sometimes said that one of the reasons the concept of policy transfer gained traction in the policy analysis literature is that it focuses on *policy change* rather than policy stability (Hudson and Lowe, 2009). This ties with a third potentially fruitful future research agenda, which is a more focused examination of how changing societal values might foster policy change. We have flagged some instances where relatively rapid change in societal values seem to have been accompanied by change in policy frameworks – for example family policy change in Ireland – but we could only scratch the surface with our account here. Significant questions remain, such as how far did changing values drive policy change and what facilitated the change in societal values. We might usefully explore countervailing trends here too, such as instances where policy frameworks have successfully resisted reform in the face of rapidly changing relevant societal values. In short, more systematic analysis of how, when and why changing societal values influence social policy change, focusing perhaps on outlier cases that buck the trend for stability, may provide important insights on the politics of policy more generally and on the conditions that facilitate path-breaking change in welfare state provision.

Note

1   See http://epp.eurostat.ec.europa.eu/portal/page/portal/microdata/eu_silc and https://www.iser.essex.ac.uk/euromod respectively.

Bibliography

Aalberg, T. (2003) *Achieving Justice: Comparative Public Opinion on Income Distribution*. Leiden: Brill.

Abrahamson, P. (1999) 'The Welfare Modelling Business', *Social Policy & Administration*, 33(4): 394–415.

Abrahamson, P. (2011) 'The Welfare Modelling Business Revisited: The Case of East Asian Welfare Regimes', in G.-J. Hwang (ed.) *New Welfare States in East Asia*, Cheltenham: Edward Elgar.

Andreβ, H.-J. and Heien, T. (2001) 'Four Worlds of Welfare State Attitudes? A Comparison of Germany, Norway, and the United States', *European Sociological Review* 17(4): 337–356.

Armingeon, K., Gerber, M., Limgruber, P., Beyeler, M. and Menegale, S. (2008) *Comparative Political Data Set 1960–2005*, Institute of Political Science, University of Berne.

Armingeon, K., Weisstanner, D., Engler, S., Potolidis, P. and Gerber, M. (2012) *Comparative Political Dataset 1960–2010,* Institute of Political Science, University of Berne, accessible at www.ipw.unibe.ch/content/team/klaus_armingeon/comparative_political_data_sets/index_ger.html.

Arts, W. and Gelissen, J. (2002) 'Three Worlds of Welfare Capitalism or More? A State-of-the-Art Report', *Journal of European Social Policy* 12(2): 137–158.

Berlant, L. (2011) *Cruel Optimism*. London: Duke University Press.

Blekesaune, M. and Quadagno, J. (2003) 'Public Attitudes toward Welfare State Policies: A Comparative Analysis of 24 Nations', *European Sociological Review* 19(5): 415–427.

Bleses, P. and Seeleib-Kaiser, M. (2004) *The Dual Transformation of the German Welfare State*. Basingstoke: Palgrave.

Bradshaw, J. and Finch, N. (2002) *A Comparison of Child Benefit Packages in 22 Countries*, Leeds: Department for Work and Pensions Research Report No. 174, Corporate Document Services.

Burstein, P. (1998) 'Bringing the Public Back In: Should Sociologists Consider the Impact of Public Opinion on Public Policy?', *Social Forces* 77(1): 27–62.

Busemeyer, M. (2013) 'Education Funding and Individual Preferences for Redistribution', *European Sociological Review* 29: 1122–1133.

Camarero, M. (2014) 'Marriage in Europe', *European Societies* 16: 443–461.

Castles, F. (1982) *The Impact of Parties. Politics and Policies in Democratic Capitalist States*. London: Sage.

Castles, F. (ed.) (1993) *Families of Nations: Patterns of Public Policy in Western Democracies*. Aldershot: Dartmouth.

Castles, F. (1996) 'Needs-Based Strategies of Social Protection in Australia and New Zealand', in G. Esping-Andersen (ed.) *Welfare States in Transition: National Adaptations in Global Economies*, London: Sage.

Castles, F. (1998) *Comparative Public Policy*. Cheltenham: Edward Elgar.

Castles, F. (2002) 'Developing New Measures of Welfare State Change and Reform', *European Journal of Political Research* 41: 613–641.

Castles, F. and Mitchell, D. (1993) 'Worlds of Welfare and Families of Nations', in F. Castles (ed.) *Families of Nations*, Aldershot: Dartmouth, 93–128.

Clasen, J. and Siegel, N. A. (eds) (2008) *Investigating Welfare State Change: The 'Dependent Variable Problem' in Comparative Analysis*. Cheltenham: Edward Elgar Publishing.

Cnaan, R. A., Hasenfeld, Y., Cnaan, A. and Rafferty, J. (1993) 'Cross-Cultural Comparison of Attitudes Toward Welfare-State Programs: Path Analysis with Log-Linear Models', *Social Indicators Research* 29: 123–152.

Cox, R. (1993) *The Development of the Dutch Welfare State: From Workers' Insurance to Universal Entitlement*. Pittsburgh: University of Pittsburgh Press.

Davie, G. (2012) 'A European Perspective on Religion and Welfare: Contrasts and Commonalities', *Social Policy and Society* 11: 589–599.

Deacon, A. (2002) *Perspectives on Welfare*. Buckingham: Open University Press.

Esping-Andersen, G. (1990) *The Three Worlds of Welfare Capitalism*. Cambridge: Polity Press.

Esping-Andersen, G. (ed.) (1996a) *Welfare States in Transition: National Adaptations in Global Economies*, London: Sage.

Esping-Andersen, G. (1996b) 'After the Golden Age? Welfare State Dilemmas in a Global Economy', in G. Esping-Andersen (ed.) *Welfare States in Transition: National Adaptations in Global Economies*, London: Sage.

Esping-Andersen, G. (1999) *The Social Foundations of Post-Industrial Economies*. Oxford: Oxford University Press.

Evans, M. (2004) 'Understanding Policy Transfer', in M. Evans (ed.) *Policy Transfer in Global Perspective*, Aldershot: Ashgate.

Evans, M. (2009) 'Policy Transfer in Critical Perspective', *Policy Studies* 30: 243–268.

Evans, M. and Davies, J. (1999) 'Understanding Policy Transfer: A Multi-Level, Multi-Disciplinary Perspective', *Public Administration* 77(2): 361–385.

EVS (2011) European Values Study 1981–2008, Longitudinal Data File. GESIS Data Archive, Cologne, Germany, ZA4804 Data File Version 2.0.0 (2011-12-30) DOI:10.4232/1.11005.

Fahey, T. and Nixon, E. (2014) 'Family Policy in Ireland', in M. Robila (ed.) *Handbook of Family Policies Across the Globe*, London: Springer.

Ferragina, E., Seeleib-Kaiser, M. and Tomlinson, M. (2013) 'Unemployment Protection and Family Policy at the Turn of the 21st Century: A Dynamic Approach to Welfare Regime Theory', *Social Policy & Administration* 47: 783–805.

Ferrara, M. (1996) 'The Southern Model of Welfare in Social Europe', *Journal of European Social Policy* 6(1): 17–37.

Flavin, P., Pacek, A. and Radcliff, B. (2011) 'State Intervention and Subjective Well-Being in Advanced Industrial Democracies', *Politics & Policy* 39: 251–269.

Flavin, P., Pacek, A. and Radcliff, B. (2014) 'Assessing the Impact of the Size and Scope of Government on Human Well-Being', *Social Forces* 92: 1241–1258.

Gelissen, J. (2008) 'European Scope-Of-Government Beliefs: The Impact of Individual, Regional and National Characteristics', in W. van Oorschot, M. Opielka and B. Pfau-Effinger (eds) *Culture and Welfare State: Values and Social Policy in Comparative Perspective*, Cheltenham: Edward Elgar.

Giger, N. (2009) 'Towards a Modern Gender Gap in Europe? A Comparative Analysis of Voting Behaviour in 12 Countries', *The Social Science Journal* 46: 474–492.

Goodin, R., Headey, R., Muffels, R. and Dirven, H. J. (1999) *The Real Worlds of Welfare Capitalism*. Cambridge: Cambridge University Press.

Goodman, R. and Peng, I. (1996) 'The East Asian Welfare States: Peripatetic Learning, Adaptive Change, and Nation-Building', in G. Esping-Andersen (ed.) *Welfare States in Transition: National Adaptations in Global Economies*, London: Sage.

Gundelach, P. (1994) 'National Value Differences: Modernization or Institutionalization?', *International Journal of Comparative Sociology* 35(1–2): 37–58.

Haller, M. (2002) 'Theory and Method in the Comparative Study of Values: Critique and Alternative to Inglehart', *European Sociological Review* 18(2): 139–158.

Häusermann, S. (2012) 'The Politics of Old and New Social Policies', in G. Bonoli and D. Natali (eds) *The Politics of the New Welfare State*, Oxford: Oxford University Press.

Hibbs, D. (1977) 'Political Parties and Macroeconomic Policy', *American Political Science Review* 71: 1467–1487.

Hitlin, S. and Piliavin, J. A. (2004) 'Values: Reviving a Dormant Concept', *Annual Review of Sociology* 30: 359–393.

Hofstede, G. (2001) *Culture's Consequences: Comparing Values, Behaviours, Institutions, and Organizations Across Nations* (2nd edition) California: Sage.

Huber, E. and Stephens, J. (2001) *Development and Crisis of the Welfare State*, Chicago: Chicago University Press.

Hudson, J. (2012) 'Welfare Regimes and Global Cities: A Missing Link in the Comparative Analysis of Welfare States?', *Journal of Social Policy* 41: 455–473.

Hudson, J. and Kühner, S. (2010) 'Beyond the Dependent Variable Problem: The Methodological Challenges of Capturing Productive and Protective Dimensions of Social Policy', *Social Policy & Society* 9(2): 167–179.

Hudson, J. and Kühner, S. (eds) (2013) 'Special Issue of Policy & Society on Theme of "Systematic Mixed Methods for Policy Analysis"', *Policy & Society* 32(4).

Hudson, J., Kühner, S. and Yang, N. (2014) 'Productive Welfare, the East Asian "Model" and Beyond: Placing Welfare Types in Greater China into Context', *Social Policy and Society* 13: 301–315.

Hudson, J. and Lowe, S. (2009) *Understanding the Policy Process*. Bristol: The Policy Press.

Inglehart, R. (1990) *Culture Shift in Advanced Industrial Society*. New Jersey: Princeton University Press.

Inglehart, R. and Norris, P. (2000) 'The Developmental Theory of the Gender Gap: Women's and Men's Voting Behaviour in Global Perspective', *International Political Science Review* 21: 441–463.

Inglehart, R. and Norris, P. (2003) *Rising Tide: Gender Equality and Cultural Change Around the World*. Cambridge: Cambridge University Press.

Jacobs, D. (2000) 'Low Public Expenditures on Social Welfare: Do East Asian Countries Have a Secret?', *International Journal of Social Welfare* 9(1): 2–16.

Jarden, A. (2011) 'An Interview with Daniel Kahneman', *International Journal of Wellbeing* 1: 186–188.

Jo, N. K. (2011) 'Between the Cultural Foundations of Welfare and Welfare Attitudes: The Possibility of an In-Between Level Conception of Culture for the Cultural Analysis of Welfare', *Journal of European Social Policy* 21(1): 5–19.

Jo, N. K. (2013) 'Social Policy and Culture: The Cases of Japan and South Korea', *Social Policy Review* 25: 167–181.

Jones, C. (1990) 'Hong Kong, Singapore, South Korea and Taiwan: Oikonomic Welfare States', *Government and Opposition* 25: 446–462.

Jones, C. (1993) 'The Pacific Challenge: Confucian Welfare Staets', in Jones, C. (ed.) *New Perspectives on the Welfare State in Europe*, London: Routledge.

Kühner, S. (2007a) *Comparative Welfare Reform Dataset 1960–2001*, accessible at www.york.ac.uk/depts/spsw/staff/kuhner.html.

Kühner, S. (2007b) 'Country-Level Comparisons of Welfare State Change Measures: Another Facet of the Dependent Variable Problem within the Comparative Analysis of the Welfare State?', *Journal of European Social Policy* 17(1): 5–18.

Kühner, S. (2013) *The Comparative Welfare Reform Dataset 1960–2010, Version II (CWRDii)*, University of York, advance access provided by author.

Kwon, H. (1998) 'Democracy and the Politics of Social Welfare: A Comparative Analysis of Welfare Systems in East Asia', *The East Asian Welfare Model: Welfare Orientalism and the State*, 23–38.

Lane, R. (2000) *The Loss of Happiness in Market Democracies*. London: Yale University Press.

Larsen, C. A. (2006) *The Institutional Logic of Welfare Attitudes: How Welfare Regimes Influence Public Support*. Aldershot: Ashgate.

Lewis, J. (1992) Gender and the Development of Welfare Regimes, *Journal of European Social Policy* 2: 159–173.

Liberini, F., Redoana, M. and Proto, E. (2013) 'Happy Voters', Centre for Competitive Advantage in the Global Economy Working Paper, University of Warwick, Working Paper No. 169, September 2013.

Lockhart, C. (2001) *Protecting the Elderly: How Culture Shapes Social Policy*. Pennsylvania: Pennsylvania State University Press.

Longest, K. and Thoits, P. (2012) 'Gender, the Stress Process, and Health: A Configurational Approach', *Society and Mental Health* 2(3): 187–206.

Longest, K. & Vaisey, S. (2008) 'Fuzzy: A Program for Performing Qualitative Comparative Analyses (QCA) in Stata', *The Stata Journal* 8(1): 79–104.

Manow, P. and Emmenegger, P. (2012) *Religion and the Gender Vote Gap: Women's Changed Political Preferences from the 1970s to 2010*. ZeS-Working Paper No. 01/2012. Bremen: Zentrum für Sozialpolitik.

Manow, P. and van Kersbergen, K. (2009) 'Religion and the Western Welfare State – The Theoretical Context', in K. van Kersbergen and P. Manow (eds) *Religion, Class Coalitions, and Welfare States*, Cambridge: Cambridge University Press.

Marklund, C. (2013) 'Introduction', in C. Marklund (ed.) *All Well in the Welfare State? Welfare, Well-Being and the Politics of Happiness*. NordWel Studies in Historical Welfare State Research 5. Helsinki: Nordic Centre of Excellence Nordwel.

Marshall, T. H. (1972) 'Value Problems of Welfare-Capitalism', *Journal of Social Policy* 1(1): 15–32.

Mathews, G. (2012) 'Happiness, Culture, and Context', *International Journal of Wellbeing* 2: 299–312.

Messner, F. (1999) 'La legislation cultuelle des pays de l'Union européenne face aux groups sectaires', in F. Champion and M. Cohen (eds), *Sectes et Démocratie*. Paris: Éditions du Seuil, pp.331–58.

Minkenberg, M. (2003) 'The Policy Impact of Church–State Relations: Family Policy and Abortion in Britain, France, and Germany', *West European Politics*, 26:1, 195–217.

Morel, N., Palier, B. and Palme, J. (2012) 'Beyond the Welfare State as We Knew It?', in N. Morel, B. Palier and J. Palme (eds) *Towards a Social Investment Welfare State? Ideas, Policies and Challenges*, Bristol: The Policy Press.

Morgan, K. (2009) 'The Religious Foundations of Work-Family Policies in Western Europe', in K. van Kersbergen and P. Manow (eds) *Religion, Class Coalitions, and Welfare States*, Cambridge: Cambridge University Press.

Myles, J. Quadango, J. (2002) 'Political Theories of the Welfare State', *Social Service Review* 76: 34–57.

Naumann, I. (2012) 'Childcare Politics in the 'New' Welfare State: Class, Religion, and Gender in the Shaping of Political Agendas', in G. Bonoli and D. Natali (eds) *The Politics of the New Welfare State*, Oxford: Oxford University Press.

O'Connor, J. S. and Robinson, G. (2008) 'Liberalism, Citizenship and the Welfare State', in W. van Oorschot, M. Opielka and B. Pfau-Effinger (eds) *Culture and Welfare State: Values and Social Policy in Comparative Perspective*, Cheltenham: Edward Elgar.

OECD (2011) *Doing Better for Families*. Paris: OECD.

OECD (2013a) *Family Policy Structures Database*. Paris: OECD Social Policy Division.

OECD (2013b) *OECD Guidelines on Measuring Subjective Well-being*. Paris: OECD.

OECD.Stat, accessible at http://stats.oecd.org/index.aspx.

Ohlsson-Wijk, S. (2011) 'Sweden's Marriage Revival: An Analysis of the New-Millennium Switch from Long-Term Decline to Increasing Popularity', *Population Studies* 65: 183–200.

Ono, H. and Lee, K.-S. (2013) 'Welfare States and the Redistribution of Happiness', *Social Forces* 92: 789–814.

Opielka, M. (2008) 'Christian Foundations of the Welfare State: Strong Cultural Values in Comparative Perspective', in W. van Oorschot, M. Opielka and B. Pfau-Effinger (eds) *Culture and Welfare State: Values and Social Policy in Comparative Perspective*, Cheltenham: Edward Elgar.

Orloff, A. (1996) 'Gender in the Welfare State', *Annual Review of Sociology* 22: 51–78.

Oyserman, D. and Uskul, A. K. (2008) 'Individualism and Collectivism: Societal-Level Processes with Implications for Individual-Level and Society-Level Outcomes', in F. J. R. van de Vijver, D. A. van Hemert and Y. H. Poortinga (eds) *Multilevel Analysis of Individuals and Cultures*, London: Lawrence Erlbaum Associates.

Pacek, A. and Radcliff, B. (2008) 'Welfare Policy and Subjective Well-Being Across Nations: An Individual-Level Assessment', *Social Research Indicators* 89: 179–191.

Page, B. I. and Shapiro, R. Y. (1983) 'Effects of Public Opinion on Policy', *The American Political Science Review* 77(1): 175–190.
Page, B. I., Shapiro, R. Y. and Dempsey, G. R. (1987) 'What Moves Public Opinion?', *The American Political Science Review* 81(1): 23–44.
Palier, B. (ed.) (2010) *A Long Goodbye to Bismarck? The Politics of Welfare Reform in Continental Europe.* Amsterdam: Amsterdam University Press.
Palier, B. (2012) 'Turning Vice into Vice: How Bismarckian Welfare States have Gone from Unsustainability to Dualization', in G. Bonoli and D. Natali (eds) *The Politics of the New Welfare State*, Oxford: Oxford University Press.
Papadopoulos, T. and Roumpakis, A. (2013) 'Familistic Welfare Capitalism in Crisis: Social Reproduction and Anti-Social Policy in Greece', *Journal of International and Comparative Social Policy* 29(3): 204–224.
Peng, I. (2002) 'Social Care in Crisis: Gender, Demography, and Welfare State Restructuring in Japan', *Social Politics* 9(3): 411–433.
Pfau-Effinger, B. (2004a) *'Culture and Path Dependency of Welfare State Development'*, Paper presented at the ESPAnet Conference 2004 (September 2004, University of Oxford), Retrieved Access at June 2013 from www.spsw.ox.ac.uk/fileadmin/static/Espanet/espanetconference/papers/ppr%5B1%5D.5.BP.pdf.
Pfau-Effinger, B. (2004b) *Development of Culture, Welfare States and Women's Employment in Europe.* Aldershot: Ashgate.
Pfau-Effinger, B. (2005) 'Culture and Welfare State Policies: Reflections on a Complex Interrelation', *Journal of Social Policy* 34(1): 3–20.
Pierson, P. (2004) *Politics in Time: History, Institutions and Social Analysis.* Oxford: Princeton University Press.
Powell, M. and Barrientos, A. (2004) 'Welfare Regimes and the Welfare Mix', *European Journal of Political Research* 43: 83–105.
Powell, M. and Barrientos, A. (2011) 'An Audit of the Welfare Modelling Business', *Social Policy & Administration* 45(1): 69–84.
Quadango, J. and Rohlinger, D. (2009) 'The Religious Factor in US Welfare State Politics', in K. van Kersbergen and P. Manow (eds) *Religion, Class Coalitions, and Welfare States*, Cambridge: Cambridge University Press.
Ragin, C. C. (2000) *Fuzzy-Set Social Science.* Chicago: University of Chicago Press.

Ragin, C. C. (2008) *Redesigning Social Inquiry: Fuzzy Sets and Beyond*. Chicago: University of Chicago Press.

Ramesh, M. and Asher, M. (2000) *Welfare Capitalism in Southeast Asia: Social Security, Health and Education Policies*. London: Macmillan.

Rieger, E. and Leibfried, S. (2003) *Limits to Globalization: Welfare States and the World Economy*. Cambridge: Polity Press in association with Blackwell.

Rihoux, B. and Ragin, C. (eds) (2008) *Configurational Comparative Methods*. London: Sage.

Rose, R. (2005) *Learning from Comparative Public Policy*. London: Routledge.

Rothstein, B. (1998) *Just Institutions Matter: The Moral and Political Logic of the Universal Welfare State*. Cambridge: Cambridge University Press.

Rothstein, B. (2010) 'Happiness and the Welfare State', *Social Research* 77: 441–468.

Schneider, C. and Wagemann, C. (2003) 'Improving Inference with a 'Two-Step' Approach: Theory and Limited Diversity in fs/QCA', European University Institute (EUI) Working Paper SPS No. 2003/7, http://www.iue.it/PUB/sps2003-07.pdf.

Schneider, C. and Wagemann, C. (2006) 'Reducing Complexity in Qualitative Comparative Analysis (QCA): Remote and Proximate Factors and the Consolidation of Democracy', *European Journal of Political Research* 45: 751–786.

Schwartz, S. H. (1992) 'Universals in the Content and Structure of Values: Theoretical Advances and Empirical Tests in 20 Countries', *Advances in Experimental Social Psychology* 25: 1–65.

Schwartz, S. H. (1994) 'Beyond Individualism/Collectivism: New Cultural Dimensions of Values', in U. Kim, H. C. Triandis, C. Kagitcibasi, S. Choi and G. Yoon (eds) *Individualism and Collectivism: Theory, Method and Applications*, London: Sage Publications.

Sjöberg, O. (2010) 'Social Insurance as a Collective Resource: Unemployment Benefits, Job Insecurity and Subjective Well-being in a Comparative Perspective', *Social Forces* 88: 1281–1304.

Skevik, A. (2006) 'Lone Motherhood in the Nordic Countries: Sole Providers in Dual-Breadwinner Regimes', in A.-L. Ellingsæter and A. Leira (eds) *Politicising Parenthood in Scandinavia*, Bristol: The Policy Press.

Stjernø, S. (2008) 'Social Democratic Values in the European Welfare States', in W. van Oorschot, M. Opielka and B. Pfau-Effinger (eds) *Culture and Welfare State: Values and Social Policy in Comparative Perspective*, Cheltenham: Edward Elgar.

Svallfors, S. (1997) 'Worlds of Welfare and Attitudes to Redistribution: A Comparison of Eight Western Nations', *European Sociological Review* 13(3): 283–304.

Svallfors, S. (2007) Class and Attitudes to Market Inequality: A Comparison of Sweden, Britain, Germany, and the United States, in S. Svallfors (ed.) *The Political Sociology of the Welfare State: Institutions, Social Cleavages, and Orientations*, California: Stanford University Press.

Tabachnick, B. G. and Fidell, L. S. (2007) *Using Multivariate Statistics* (5th edition) London: Pearson Education.

Taylor-Gooby, P. (ed.) (2004a) *New Risks, New Welfare: The Transformation of the European Welfare State*. Oxford: Oxford University Press.

Taylor-Gooby, P. (2004b) 'New Social Risks and Welfare States: New Paradigm and New Politics?', in P. Taylor-Gooby, (ed.) *New Risks, New Welfare: The Transformation of the European Welfare State*, Oxford: Oxford University Press.

Therborn, G. (1989) "Pillarization' and 'Popular Movements'. Two Variants of Welfare State Capitalism: the Netherlands and Sweden', in F. Castles (ed.) *The Comparative History of Public Policy*, Cambridge: Polity Press.

Thiem, A. and Dusa, A. (2013) 'QCA: A Package for Qualitative Comparative Analysis', *The R Journal* 5(1): 87–97.

Titmuss, R. M. (1974) *Social Policy*. London: Allen & Unwin.

Twisk, J. W. R. (2006) *Applied Multilevel Analysis*. Cambridge: Cambridge University Press.

van de Vijver, F. J. R., van Hemert, D. A. and Poortinga, Y. H. (2008) 'Conceptual Issues in Multilevel Models', in F. J. R. van de Vijver, D. A. van Hemert and Y. H. Poortinga (eds) *Multilevel Analysis of Individuals and Cultures*, London: Lawrence Erlbaum Associates.

van Kersbergen, K. (1995) *Social Capitalism*. London: Routledge.

van Kersbergen, K. and Kremer, M. (2008) 'Conservatism and the Welfare State: Intervening to Preserve', in W. van Oorschot, M. Opielka and B. Pfau-Effinger (eds) *Culture and Welfare State*, Cheltenham: Edward Elgar.

van Kersbergen, K. and Manow, P. (eds) (2009) *Religion, Class Coalitions, and Welfare States*. Cambridge: Cambridge University Press.

van Oorschot, W. (2000) 'Who Should Get What, and Why? On Deservingness Criteria and the Conditionality of Solidarity Among the Public', *Policy & Politics* 28(1): 33–48.

van Oorschot, W. (2006) 'Making the Difference in Social Europe: Deservingness Perceptions among Citizens of European Welfare States', *Journal of European Social Policy* 16(1): 23–42.

van Oorschot, W. (2007) 'Culture and Social Policy: A Developing Field of Study', *International Journal of Social Welfare* 16(2): 129–39.

van Oorschot, W. (2008) 'Popular Deservingness Perceptions and Conditionality of Solidarity in Europe', in W. van Oorschot, M. Opielka and B. Pfau-Effinger (eds) *Culture and Welfare State: Values and Social Policy in Comparative Perspective*, Cheltenham: Edward Elgar.

van Oorschot, W. and Halman, L. (2000) 'Blame or Fate, Individual or Social? An International Comparison of Popular Explanations of Poverty', *European Societies* 2(1): 1–28.

Veenhoven, R. (1987) 'Cultural Bias in Ratings of Perceived Life Quality: A Comments on Ostroot & Snijder', *Social Indicators Research* 19: 329–334.

Veenhoven, R. (2000) 'Well-being in the Welfare State: Level not Higher, Distribution Not More Equitable', *Journal of Comparative Policy Analysis: Research and Practice* 2: 91–125.

Veenhoven, R. (2012) 'Cross-National Differences in Happiness: Cultural Measurement Bias or Effect of Culture?', *International Journal of Wellbeing* 2: 333–353.

Walker, A. and Wong, C. K. (2005) 'Conclusion: From Confucianism to Globalisation', in Alan Walker and Chack-Kie Wong (eds) *East Asian Welfare Regimes in Transition: From Confucianism to Globalisation*, Bristol: Policy Press.

White, G. and Goodman, R. (1998) 'Welfare Orientalism and the Search for an East Asian Welfare Model', *The East Asian welfare model: Welfare Orientalism and the State*, 3–24.

Wildeboer Schut, J. M., Vrooman, J. C. and de Beer, P. (2001) *On Worlds of Welfare. Institutions and Their Effects in Eleven Welfare States*. The Hague: Social and Cultural Planning Office of the Netherlands.

Wuthnow, R. (1989) *Communities of Discourse*. Cambridge, MA: Harvard University Press.

WVS (2009) World Value Survey 1981–2008 official aggregate v.20090901, 2009. World Values Survey Association (www.worldvaluessurvey.org). Aggregate File Producer: ASEP/JDS, Madrid.

Index

abortion, 16, 22, 89–91
affective environment, 103–4
Australia, 8, 47n1, 61
  cluster analysis, 19, 20
  cluster subgrouping, 87, 88
  Liberal regime, 85, 86
Austria, 47n1, 66
  cluster analysis, 19, 20
  Conservative/Corporatist regime, 78, 79, 81

Belgium, 47n1, 66
  cluster analysis, 19, 20
  Conservative/Corporatist regime, 78, 79, 81
Blair, Tony, 61

cabinet composition, 48n8
  family policy expenditure, 37, 38, 39–40, 41, 43
  unemployment expenditure, 28, 29, 30, 34
Canada, 47n1
  cluster analysis, 19, 20
  cluster subgrouping, 87, 88
  Liberal regime, 85, 86
Catholic Church, 60, 66
Catholic values, 48n7, 89–90
childcare policies, 40, 58, 82, 85
Christian Democrat, 48n7, 51, 63, 66, 85
Church, family policy, 8, 39, 47–8n7

Clark, Helen, 61
cluster analysis of societal values, 19, 20
  Conservative/Corporatist regime, 79, 81
  Liberal regime, 86, 88–91
Comparative Political Data Set, 14, 25
comparative social policy analysis, bringing culture back in, 111–13
Comparative Welfare Reform Dataset, 14, 25
Confucian model of welfare, 9
conservatism index
  scores by cluster analysis, 81
  scores by regime, 82, 83
Conservative/Corporatist regime, 3–4, 19, 21, 47n1
  cluster analysis of societal values, 79, 81
  conservatism index, 82, 83
  dissolving of socially conservative values, 84–5
  family policy spending, 58, 64–7
  puzzle in exploring family policy, 78–85
  social expenditure on family policy, 38, 39, 41, 43
  social expenditure on unemployment, 30, 34
  unemployment spending, 33

126 Index

conservative social norms
  cluster analysis for Conservative/
    Corporatist regime, 81
  cluster analysis for Liberal regime,
    86
  cultural factor, 28
  family policy expenditure, 37, 38,
    41, 43
  social expenditure on
    unemployment, 29, 30, 34
  societal value, 22, 68
  unemployment spending, 29, 30, 31,
    33, 35
Cruel Optimism (Berlant), 32
cultural and political legacies, 8
cultural context
  family policy expenditure, 35–45
  societal values, 16–18
  unemployment expenditure, 27–35
culture
  bringing back in to comparative
    social policy analysis, 111–13
  conceptualising, 10–12
  cross-national variations in welfare,
    21
  exploring, and welfare, 6–7
  notion of, 2
  welfare modeling, 7–10
culture-welfare nexus
  limits of quantitative analysis,
    50–2
  qualitative analysis methods, 52–7
  quantitative analysis, 25–7
  see also qualitative analysis

Denmark, 47*n*1
  cluster analysis, 19, 20
  traditional family values, 59, 92,
    94–5, 96
distant factors
  qualitative analysis, 55
  three-step fsQCA, 53
  welfare regime effects, 57–59
  see also fsQCA (fuzzy-set qualitative
    comparative analysis)
divorce, 16, 22, 89, 92

East Asian regime, 65
  cluster analysis, 19, 20
  conservatism index, 82, 83, 84
  welfare model, 8, 9, 18, 19
European Social Survey, 99
European Values Study (EVS), 2, 6,
  12–17, 25, 45, 47*n*2, 63, 72, 88, 92,
  94–8, 100, 107, 109, 111
euthanasia, 16, 22

families of nations, 9
family policy, 47–8*n*7
  care-welfare nexus, 26
  cultural context and, expenditure,
    35–45
  maternity leave policies, 42, 43, 44
  social expenditure on, 37, 38, 41
family policy spending
  Conservative/Corporatist regime,
    64–7, 78–85
  Ireland, 89
  Liberal regime, 60–4
  puzzling features in analysis,
    69–70
  Social Democratic regime, 59–60
  Southern European regime, 59–60
  welfare regime effects, 57–9
Family Policy Structures Database
  (OECD), 25
family values, 28, *see also* traditional
  family values
female labour participation rate, 25,
  36, 61
  family policy expenditure, 37, 38,
    41, 43
Finland, 47*n*1
  cluster analysis, 19, 20
  traditional family values, 92, 94–5,
    96
France, 47*n*1, 66
  cluster analysis, 19, 20
  Conservative/Corporatist regime,
    78, 79, 81, 84
fsQCA (fuzzy-set qualitative
  comparative analysis), 3, 50–2,
  67–70, 107–8

DOI: 10.1057/9781137457493.0012

fsQCA – *continued*
  Conservative/Corporatist regime, 64–7
  constraints on approach, 74–5n4
  creating scores for QCA sets, 51
  creating sets and identifying pathways, 54–5, 57
  factors and outcomes in three-step, 53
  Liberal regime, 60–4
  methods, 52–7, 70–1
  overview of approach, 52–4
  set calibration, 71–2
  set relations, 72–4
  Social Democratic regime, 59–60
  software usage, 72
  Southern European regime, 59–60
  three-step approach, 56, 67–8
  variants of approach, 74n1
  welfare regime effects overall, 57–9

GDP (gross domestic product), 25, 27, 99
  social expenditure on family (as % GDP), 37, 38
  social expenditure on unemployment (as % GDP), 29, 30
GDP growth rate, social expenditure on unemployment, 28, 29
GDP per capita, 27
  family policy expenditure, 37, 38, 41, 43
  unemployment expenditure, 30, 34
gendered welfare regimes, 75n12
German welfare state, 82, 85
Germany, 47n1
  classification, 80, 82
  cluster analysis, 19, 20
  Conservative/Corporatist regime, 79, 81
Google Scholar, 6, 23n1
Greece, 47n1
  cluster analysis, 19, 20
  traditional family values, 94, 98

happiness-culture debate, optimistic values, 102–3

IMF (International Monetary Fund), 25
in-between level approach, culture, 2, 11–12, 21, 105, 107–9
intermediate factors
  calibration, 71
  Conservative/Corporatist regime, 65
  Liberal regime, 61–2
  qualitative analysis, 55, 56
  Social Democratic regime, 59–60
  Southern European regime, 59–60
  three-step fsQCA, 53
  see also fsQCA (fuzzy-set qualitative comparative analysis)
International Social Survey Program, 100
inter-personal tolerance
  family policy expenditure, 37
  social expenditure on unemployment, 28, 29, 30, 32, 34
  societal value, 22
  unemployment as % of GDP, 29
Ireland, 47n1
  abortion, 89–91
  changing family policy, 88–90
  cluster analysis, 19, 20
  cluster subgrouping, 87, 88
  family policy expenditures, 89
  Liberal regime, 85, 86
Italy, 47n1
  cluster analysis, 19, 20
  traditional family values, 94, 98

Japan, 8, 19, 20, 65, 82

Liberal regime, 47n1
  bifurcation, 4, 65, 78, 85–91, 105n4, 108
  cluster analysis for societal values, 86
  conservatism index, 82, 83, 85, 88
  family policy spending, 39, 58, 75n9
life satisfaction, 99–100
lone parenthood, 95, 96, 97–8

Luxembourg, 47*n*1
  cluster analysis, 19, 20
  Conservative/Corporatist regime, 78, 79, 81

macro-level approach, culture, 2, 10–11
marriage, traditional views of, 92, 94–5, 96, 97
maternity leave, family policy structures, 42, 43, 44
micro-level approach, culture, 2, 11
multilevel models (MLM), 47*n*2

Netherlands, 29, 47*n*1
  classification, 80
  cluster analysis, 19, 20
  Conservative/Corporatist regime, 66, 78, 79, 80, 81
New Zealand, 8, 9, 47*n*1, 61
  cluster analysis, 19, 20
  cluster subgrouping, 87, 88
  Liberal regime, 85, 86
Norway, 47*n*1
  cluster analysis, 19, 20
  traditional family values, 59, 92, 95, 96, 97

OECD (Organisation for Economic Co-operation and Development), 7, 29, 42, 75*n*11, 95, 97
  countries, 13, 92, 100
  nations, 23
  optimistic values scores by country, 101
  SOCX database, 14, 25, 44
  traditional family values by country, 93
OLS (ordinary least squares) regression models, 28, 47*n*2
  generosity of maternity leave, 43
  social expenditure on family policy, 38, 41
  social expenditure on unemployment, 30, 34
optimism
  post-war, 32, 103
  societal value, 14
optimistic values, 4, 22, 27
  cultural factor, 28
  good life, 104–5
  happiness-culture debate, 102–3
  life satisfaction and state size, 99–100
  scores by country over time, 101
  social expenditure on family policy, 37
  social expenditure on unemployment, 29, 30, 34
  social policy and, 104
  subjective well-being, 31, 99, 102–4
  unemployment spending, 30, 31–2

parenthood, lone, 95, 96, 97–8
pathways
  identifying, 55, 73
  summary of solution, 74
permissive values on adherence to laws
  family policy expenditure, 37
  social expenditure on unemployment, 28, 29
  societal value, 22
policy feedback, 98, 103–4, 105, 108
political activeness, 79
  social expenditure on family, 36, 37
  social expenditure on unemployment, 28, 29
  societal value, 17, 22
political orientedness, 79
  social expenditure on family, 36, 37
  social expenditure on unemployment, 28, 29
  societal value, 17, 22
political participation and citizenship, 17
Portugal, 47*n*1
  cluster analysis, 19, 20
  traditional family values, 59, 98
proximate factors
  calibration, 72
  Conservative/Corporatist regime, 65
  Liberal regime, 61–2
  qualitative analysis, 55, 56

proximate factors – *continued*
 Social Democratic regime, 59–60
 Southern European regime, 59–60
 three-step fsQCA, 53
 see also fsQCA (fuzzy-set qualitative comparative analysis)

Qualitative Comparative Analysis (QCA), 17, 22, 57, 67, 73, 74n2
 crisp set (csQCA), 50, 51, 74n1
 factors and outcomes in three-step fsQCA, 53
 methods, 52–7
 overview of approach, 52–4
 see also fsQCA (fuzzy-set qualitative comparative analysis)

regression models, 3, 47n2, 84, 107
 exploring culture and welfare, 25–7
 family policy, 37–9, 42–4, 64, 80
 fsQCA to supplement, 51–2, 80, 84, 105
 multi-level, 110–11
 unemployment policy, 28, 31, 35, 46
religiosity, 28
 cluster analysis for Conservative/Corporatist regime, 81
 cluster analysis for Liberal regime, 85, 86
 social expenditure on family policy, 37, 38, 41, 43, 63
 social expenditure on unemployment, 28, 29
 societal value, 14, 22, 68
remote factors
 Conservative/Corporatist regime, 65
 Liberal regime, 62
 qualitative analysis, 56
 Social Democratic regime, 60
 Southern European regime, 60

social conservatism, 80, 82, 85, 90, 92, 105n4
Social Democratic regime, 47n1
 conservatism index, 82, 83
 expansive family policy, 107

family policy, 44, 46, 57
 social expenditure on family policy, 38, 39, 41, 43
 social expenditure on unemployment, 30, 34
 unemployment spending, 33
 welfare, 18, 19
Social Foundations of Post-Industrial Economies (Esping-Andersen), 8
social insurance, family, 47–8n7
societal values, 2
 bringing culture back, 111–13
 capturing, 109–10
 cluster analysis, 20
 cluster analysis of, 19
 cultural context, 16–18
 examples of extracted, 22
 fusing multi-method, multi-disciplinary, multi-level approaches, 110–11
 identifying, 16–18
 identifying stable, 12–16
 in-between approach, 12–16
 process for extracting examples of, 15
 quantitative analyses of culture and welfare, 25–7
 regression models, 3
software, *fuzzy* program, 72
Southern European regime, 47n1
 conservatism index, 83, 84
 family policy spending, 57–8
 social expenditure on family policy, 38, 41, 43
 social expenditure on unemployment, 30, 34
 traditional family values, 98
 unemployment spending, 32–3
 welfare, 19, 21
South Korea, 2
 East Asian welfare, 8, 82
 cluster analysis, 19, 20
Spain, 47n1
 cluster analysis, 19, 20
 traditional family values, 59, 98

subjective well-being (SWB), 31, 99, 102–4
Sweden, 47n1
  cluster analysis, 19, 20
  traditional family values, 92, 94–5, 96, 97–8
Switzerland, 47n1
  cluster analysis, 19, 20
  cluster subgrouping, 87, 88
  Liberal regime, 85, 86

Three Worlds of Welfare Capitalism, The (Esping-Andersen), 7, 8, 26
tolerance, 14, 28, 32, *see also* interpersonal tolerance
traditional cultural framework, 8
traditional family values, 4, 14, 27
  cluster analysis for Conservative/Corporatist regime, 81
  cluster analysis for Liberal regime, 86
  lone parenthood, 95, 96, 97–8
  marriage, 92, 94–5, 96, 97
  scores by country over time, 93
  Social Democratic regime, 92, 94–8
  Social expenditure on family policy, 37, 38, 41, 43
  social expenditure on unemployment, 29, 30, 34
  societal value, 22, 69
  Southern European regime, 98
  unemployment spending, 35

unemployment
  as percentage of GDP, 28–9, 30
  social expenditure on, 29, 30, 34
  variables for regression models, 28
  work-welfare nexus, 26
unemployment rate, 27, 36
  family policy expenditure, 37, 38, 41, 43
  unemployment expenditure, 29, 30, 34
union density, 25, 28, 36, 55
  family policy expenditure, 37, 38, 41, 43, 44
  unemployment expenditure, 29, 30, 33, 34
United Kingdom (UK), 2, 19, 20, 47n1, 61, 63, 68, 85, 104
  cluster analysis, 19, 20
  cluster subgrouping, 87, 88
  Liberal regime, 85, 86
United States, 47n1, 61, 63, 68
  cluster analysis, 19, 20
  cluster subgrouping, 87, 88
  Liberal regime, 85, 86

welfare, exploring culture and, 6–7
welfare culture approach, 10, 12, 25
welfare modeling, culture and, 7–10
Welfare States in Transition (Esping-Andersen), 8
welfare types, embeddedness of culture in, 18–21
World Values Survey (WVS), 2, 6, 12–17, 23n7, 25, 42, 47n2, 63, 72, 88, 94–100, 107, 109, 111